MYSTERY OF THE AGES

by Mel Bond

Mystery of the Ages

PO Box 306
140 N. Point Prairie
Wentzville, MO 63385

Printed in the United States of America

ISBN 978-1882318-06-3

Unless otherwise indicated, all Scripture quotations are taken from the King James Version of the Bible or prominent Hebrew and Greek concordances.

Deuteronomy 29:29

"The secret things belong unto the Lord our God: BUT those things which are revealed BELONG UNTO US AND TO OUR CHILDREN FOREVER, THAT WE MANY DO ALL THE WORDS OF THIS LAW!" (The Hebrew word for "revealed" is *galah*, which is co-equally rendered *plainly published*.)

CONTENTS

INTRODUCTION

MYSTERY OF THE AGES, NOW MADE KNOWN

Most Christians have missed the great blessings of God in this world by not knowing the truths of what God has already supplied. Many Christians spend years praying and even fasting with the motive of trying to get God to do something for them, yet never see their petitions manifest. In fact, often times their situation only worsens.

So many people waste years of their life wanting God to do something sensational to make this life better for them. So they continue to wait, year after year, for something sensational (such as an angel to appear to them, or an audible voice from God, or some great ministry to come their way to give them a word from God), when God has already given them all things that pertain to this life and Godliness! God has already supernaturally supplied all things for us.

Sensational things are things of the senses, the things of which the flesh can relate. The supernatural is the Godly divine, spiritual realm of God's Word.

In Mark 9:2-8, Jesus took Peter, James and John with Him to a mountain to pray. As they were praying, James and John witnessed Moses and Elijah appear and speak to Jesus. Shortly afterwards, a cloud overshadowed them and out of it a voice spoke saying, "This is My beloved Son in Whom I am well pleased."

By the inspiration of the Holy Spirit, Peter drew attention to the fact that God's Word is *more* sure than even the appearance of angels and supernatural manifestations (such as God speaking through a cloud) (see II Peter 1:16-21; Mark 9:2-8).

I've found 700+ verses in the New Testament that tell us that God has already given us everything we could ever need or desire. All of these verses are facts from the heart of God that belong to us because of Jesus. When Jesus died on the cross, He paid the price so that everything that pertains to this life and God-likeness would be ours!

II Peter 1:3, "According as His divine power HATH given unto us ALL things that pertain unto life and **Godliness**, through the knowledge of Him that hath called us to **glory** and **virtue**." (In this passage, the Greek word for "Godliness" is *eusebeia*, which is co-equally rendered *Godly, divine*. The Greek word for "glory" is *doxa*, which is co-equally rendered *a thing belonging to God, excellence of Christ, the reputation of*

God. The Greek word for "virtue" is *arête*, which is co-equally rendered *excellence.*)

Romans 8:32 is another example that validates this doctrine, "He (God) that spared not His own Son, but delivered Him up for us all, how shall He not with Him also freely give us ALL things?"

Most Christians believe the first part of the verse, but not the second part. However, if the second part is not true, then the first part is not true, either. But both are true!

There are 103 verses in New Testament that use the Greek word *sozo*. In our English Bibles, this word is written as *salvation, healing, wholeness, prosperity, deliverance, safety.*

There are 68 times in the New Testament that the Greek word *aitoe* is used. In our modern day Bibles it is written *ask* or *desire*. The fuller meaning of this word in the Greek is *to strictly demand something due, to crave or require.*

As you read these Scriptures, keep in mind that we are strictly demanding what it due us from satan. God already gave it to us, satan stole it, and we must strictly demand it back.

In the New Testament, there are 144 verses that tell us who we are, what we can do, and what we have because of Christ. These verses give validity to the fact that God has already given us everything we could ever need or desire.

In the New Testament there are 260 verses with various phrasings, yet they all convey the same message "that God has already given us everything we could ever need or desire".

CHAPTER 1

ZOE

There are 126 verses in the New Testament in which the Greek word *zoe* is used and translated as *life* in our English Bibles. This Greek word *zoe* is co-equally rendered *life the way God has it, the God kind of life, absolute fullness of life, both essential and ethical which belongs to God, even in this world who put their trust in Christ.*

Out of these 126 verses, 87 of them tell us that Jesus paid the price, so that we would have *zoe* now in this life.

Matthew 7:14, "Because strait is the gate, and narrow is the way, which leadeth unto **life** *(zoe)*, and few there be that **find** it." (In this passage, the Greek word for "find" is *heurisko*, which is co-equally rendered *obtain*.)

God gave *zoe*, we must find it. One would need to search the Scriptures and act on them to "find it".

Matthew 19:17, "...If thou wilt enter into **life** *(zoe)*, keep the commandments."

This passage is telling us that God has done His part, and if we want *zoe*, then our part is to keep the commandments.

Matthew 19:29, "...and every one that hath forsaken houses or brethren, or sisters, or father or mother, or wife, or children or lands, for My name's sake, shall receive a hundredfold, and shall inherit everlasting **life** *(zoe)*."

Mark 10:17, "...what shall I do that I may **inherit** eternal **life** (*zoe*)?" (In this passage, the Greek word for "inherit" is *kleronomeo*, which is co-equally rendered *obtain, share, possess.*)

In verse 19, Jesus answered "...know the commandments."

God has already given *zoe*, we must do our part by knowing God's Word.

Mark 10:30, "...But he shall receive a hundredfold now in this time ... and in the world **to come** eternal **life** *(zoe)*." (In this passage, the Greek word for the phrase "to come" is *erchomai*, which is co-equally rendered *appear, accompany, come, enter, to be set.*)

So, a more accurate translation would be, "...come enter this eternal **life**" (see Matthew 19:17).

Luke 10:25-27, "...a certain lawyer stood up, and tempted him, saying, Master, what shall I do to inherit eternal **life** *(zoe)*? He said unto him, what is written in the law? How readest thou? And He answering said, Thou shalt love the Lord thy God with all thy heart, and with all thy soul, and with all thy strength, and with all thy mind; and thy neighbor as thyself. And He said unto him, Thou hast answered right: this do and thou shalt **live**." (In this passage, the Greek word for "live" is *zao*, which is the root word for *zoe.*)

Luke 18:30, "...who shall not receive manifold more in this present time, and in the world **to come life** *(zoe)* everlasting." (In this passage, the Greek word for the phrase "to come" is the same as used in Mark 10:30, rendered *come enter this eternal life.*)

John 3:15-16, "...that whosoever believeth in Him should not perish, but have eternal **life** *(zoe)*. For God so loved the world, that He gave His only begotten Son, that whosoever believeth in Him should not perish, but have everlasting **life** *(zoe)*."

God gave. Therefore, if we believe, we have *zoe*.

John 3:36, "...He that believeth on the Son hath everlasting **life** *(zoe)*."

John 4:14, "...the water that I shall give him shall be in him a well of water springing up into everlasting **life** *(zoe)*."

Romans 5:18, "Therefore as by the offence of one judgment came upon all men to condemnation; even so by the righteousness of One the free gift came upon all men unto justification of **life** *(zoe)*."

Jesus came and paid the price for us to have *zoe,* now, in this life.

Romans 5:21, "...that as sin hath reigned unto death, even so might grace reign through righteousness unto eternal **life** *(zoe)* by Jesus Christ our Lord."

John 5:24, "...heareth My word, and believeth on Him that sent Me, hath everlasting **life** *(zoe)*, and shall not come into condemnation; but is passed from death unto **life** *(zoe)*."

The simplicity of having *zoe* is hearing and believing the Word. The Word has already been given; all we need to do is receive it.

Romans 6:4, "Therefore we are buried with Him by baptism into death: that like as Christ was raised up from the dead by the glory of the Father, even so we also **should walk** in newness of **life** *(zoe).*" (In this passage, the Greek word for the phrase "should walk" is *peripateo,* which is co-equally rendered *walk at large, especially as proof of ability, be occupied with.*)

Romans 6:23, "For the wages of sin is death; but the gift of God is eternal **life** *(zoe)* through Jesus Christ our Lord."

We have all sinned and deserve death; however, because we have made Jesus Christ our Lord, we are now exempt from the wages, and instead, we get *zoe.*

John 6:33, "...the bread of God is He which cometh down from Heaven, and giveth **life** *(zoe)* unto the world."

John 6:40, "...this is the will of Him that sent Me, that every one which **seeth** the Son, and believeth on Him, may have everlasting **life** *(zoe).*" (In this passage, the Greek word for "seeth" is *theoreo,* which is co-equally rendered *experience, acknowledge, consider, perceive.*)

John 6:47, "...He that believeth on Me hath everlasting **life** *(zoe).*"

John 6:51, "I am the living bread which came down from Heaven: if any man eat of this bread, he shall live forever: and the bread that I will give is My flesh, which I will give for the **life** *(zoe)* of the world."

John 6:54, "...whoso eateth My flesh, and drinketh My blood, hath eternal **life** *(zoe)*."

John 6:63, "It is the Spirit that **quickeneth**, the flesh profiteth nothing: the words that I speak unto you, they are spirit, and they are **life** *(zoe)*." (In this passage, the Greek word for "quickeneth" is *zoopoieo*, which is co-equally rendered *make alive, give life*.)

According to God's Word, things that are promised are made alive in this natural world.

John 6:68, "...thou hast the words of eternal **life** *(zoe)*."

Romans 8:2, "...for the law of the spirit of **life** *(zoe)* in Christ Jesus hath made me free from the law of sin and death."

Romans 8:6, "...for to be carnally minded is death; but to be spiritually minded is **life** *(zoe)* and peace."

Again, the decision is ours. Even though *zoe* is ours, if we choose to be carnally minded, we will not experience it.

Romans 8:10, "...and if Christ be in you, the body is dead because of sin; but the spirit is **life** *(zoe)* because of righteousness."

John 8:12, "Then spake Jesus ... he that followeth Me shall not walk in darkness, but shall have the light of **life** *(zoe)*."

John 10:10, "I am come that they might have **life** *(zoe)*, and that they might have it more abundantly."

John 10:28, "And I give unto them eternal **life** *(zoe)*..."

John 14:6, "Jesus saith unto him, I am the way, the truth, and the **life** *(zoe)*..."

John 20:31, "But these are written, that ye might believe that Jesus is the Christ, the Son of God; and that believing ye might have **life** *(zoe)* through His name."

Romans 5:17, "For if by one man's offence death reigned by one; much more they which receive abundance of grace and of the gift of righteousness shall reign in **life** *(zoe)* by One, Jesus Christ."

I Corinthians 3:22, "...**life** *(zoe)* or death, or things present, or things to come; all are yours."

II Corinthians 3:6, "...Who also hath made us able ministers of the New Testament; not of the letter, but of the Spirit: for the letter killeth, but the Spirit giveth **life** *(zoe)*."

The following several verses, refer to *zoe* as being in our natural bodies.

II Corinthians 4:10, "Always bearing about in the body the dying of the Lord Jesus, that the **life** *(zoe)* also of Jesus might be made manifest in our body."

II Corinthians 4:11, "For we which live are always delivered unto death for Jesus, that the **life** *(zoe)* also of Jesus might be made manifest in our mortal flesh."

II Corinthians 5:4, "For we which live are always delivered unto death for Jesus sake, that the **life** *(zoe)* also of Jesus might be made manifest in our mortal flesh."

Galatians 6:8, "For he that soweth to his flesh shall of the flesh reap corruption; but he that soweth to the spirit shall of the spirit reap **life** *(zoe)* everlasting."

If we want the *zoe* that is already given to us, we must put it on by sowing to the spirit. We must make efforts to put God's Word in our lives.

Ephesians 4:18, "Having the understanding darkened, being alienated from the **life** *(zoe)* of God through the ignorance that is in them, because of the blindness of their heart."

If we want this *zoe* to be in our life, we must allow God's Word to open our understanding. Psalm 119:130 says, "(God's) words give light; (they) give understanding to the simple."

I Timothy 4:8, "For bodily exercise profiteth little: but Godliness is profitable unto all things, having promise of the **life** *(zoe)* that now is, and of that which is to come."

Godliness allows the *zoe* that has been given to manifest in our natural lives.

I Timothy 6:12, "Fight the good fight of faith, lay hold on eternal **life** *(zoe)*, whereunto thou art also called, and hast professed a good profession before many witnesses."

I Timothy 6:19, "Laying up in store for themselves a good foundation against the time to come, that they may lay hold on eternal **life** *(zoe)*."

II Timothy 1:1, "Paul, an apostle of Jesus Christ by the will of God, according to the promise of **life** *(zoe)* which is in Christ Jesus."

II Timothy 1:10, "But is now made manifest by the appearing of our Savior Jesus Christ, Who hath abolished death, and hath brought **life** *(zoe)* and immortality to light through the Gospel."

James 1:12, "Blessed is the man that endured temptation: for when he is tried, he shall receive the crown of **life** *(zoe)*, which the Lord hath promised to them that love Him."

We must initiate endurance, so we can experience *zoe* in this life.

I Peter 3:10, "For he that will love **life** *(zoe)*, and see good days, let him refrain his tongue from **evil**, and his lips that they speak no **guile**." (In this passage, the Greek word for "evil" is *kakos*, which is co-equally rendered *worthless, injurious*. The Greek word for "guile" is *dolos*, which is co-equally rendered *trick, deceit*.)

God has given this life; however, for us to receive it, we must follow the directions of how to receive.

II Peter 1:3, "According as his divine power hath given unto us all things that pertain unto **life** *(zoe)* and Godliness, through the knowledge of Him that hath called us to glory and virtue."

I John 1:2, "For the **life** *(zoe)* was **manifested**, and we have seen it, and bear witness, **and show** unto you that eternal **life** *(zoe)*, which was with the Father, and was **manifested** unto us." (In this passage, the Greek word for the phrase "and show" is *apaggellō*, which is co-equally rendered *to declare, complete*. Also, both times the word "manifested" appears in this verse, it is the Greek word *phaneroo*, which is co-equally rendered *declare*.)

I John 2:25, "And this is the promise **that He hath promised** us, even eternal **life** *(zoe).*" (In this passage, the Greek word for the phrase "that He hath promised" is *epaggello,* which is co-equally rendered *to announce upon, to- bring tidings, by implication, a pastor/angel.*)

God has given us His *zoe,* and as we apply the truths of receiving this life, angels cause it to be brought to us (see Galatians 3:19).

I John 3:14-15, "**We know** that we have passed from death unto **life** *(zoe)***,** because we love the brethren. He that loveth not his brother abideth in death." (In this passage, the Greek word for the phrase "we know" is *eido,* which is co-equally rendered *to experience.*)

There is a supernatural experience of *zoe* when a person begins to have unconditional love for others.

I John 5:11, "And this is the record, that God hath given to us eternal **life** *(zoe),* and this **life** *(zoe)* is in His Son."

I John 5:12, "He that hath the Son hath **life** *(zoe)*; and he that hath not the Son of God hath not **life** *(zoe).*"

When a person accepts the Lord Jesus Christ into their heart, something very supernatural and divine takes place; *zoe* takes place. I Corinthians 2:14 tells us that the natural person does not understand the things of God, for they are foolishness to him. Once a person is born-again, they can begin to understand the Word of God and God, Himself. Their way of thinking begins to change. They start seeing and understanding things from God's standpoint. Real *zoe* takes place.

I John 5:13, "These things have I written unto you that believe on the name of the Son of God; that ye may know that ye have eternal life *(zoe)*, and that ye may believe on the name of the Son of God."

When we who are born-again read the Word of God, a knowing of *zoe* takes place in our lives. The more we read, the more we experience, the more we know we have *zoe*!

Revelation 21:6, "And He said unto me, it is done. I am the Alpha and Omega, the beginning and the end. I will give unto him that is athirst of the fountain of the water of **life** *(zoe)* freely."

For further study, please read the following verses that show we have *zoe* in this life:

Matthew 7:14; 17:29
Mark 10:21, 30
Luke 1:75; 10:25; 18:18, 30
John 1:4; 4:36; 5:40; 6:27, 33, 35, 47, 51, 53-54; 10:27-28; 11:25; 17:2
Acts 2:28; 5:20; 11:18; 13:46, 48
Romans 6:22; 8:10
I Corinthians 15:19
II Corinthians 2:16; 4:12
Philippians 1:20; 2:16; 4:3
Colossians 3:3; 4
I Timothy 1:16; 6:12
II Timothy 1:1, 10
Titus 1:12
I John 1:1; 2:25; 5:11, 20
Jude 1:21

Revelation 22:17, "And the spirit and the bride say, Come, and let him that heareth say, Come. And let him that is athirst come. And whosoever will, let him take the water of **life** *(zoe)* freely."

God is not a tyrant. He does not force anyone to accept His divine life; they must want Him!

CHAPTER 2

SOZO & SOTERIA

In this chapter, we are going to study the Greek words *sozo* and *soteria*. The Greek word *soteria* is the foundation word for *sozo*. Most of the time, *sozo* is translated as *save* or *saved,* and *soteria* is translated as *salvation.*

In the Greek, the fuller meaning of *sozo* is *save, make whole, heal, keep safe, rescue from danger, protect, do well.* This Greek word is used 103 times in the New Testament. Most of the time this word is used, it shows that we have *sozo*, right now, in this natural life, because of the price that Jesus paid on the cross.

There are 42 verses in the New Testament that use the Greek word *soteria*. The fuller meaning of this word is *deliver, health, do well, make whole.*

THE STUDY OF SOZO

(save)

Matthew 1:21, "And she shall bring forth a son, and thou shalt call His name Jesus: for He shall **save** *(sozo)* His people from their **sins**." (In this passage, the Greek word for "sins" is *hamartia*, which is co-equally rendered *to miss the mark, faults, offense.)*

So, this portion of this verse could be translated, "...His name Jesus: for He shall bring wholeness, safety, wellness and healing in every area of life for His people from their faults, offense and missing what belongs to them."

Matthew 14:30, "But when he saw the wind boisterous, he was afraid; and beginning to sink, he cried, saying, Lord, **save** (*sozo*) me. And immediately Jesus stretched forth His hand, and caught him, and said **unto him, O thou of little faith**, wherefore didst thou doubt? And when they were come into the ship, the wind ceased." (In this passage, the Greek word for the phrase "unto him, O thou of little faith" is *oligopistos*, which is co-equally rendered *lacking confidence, to yield, believe or trust.*)

Peter knew that having *sozo* would allow him to walk on water, and Jesus told him that if he had only a little confidence to yield and trust in God's Word, he could walk on water.

Matthew 18:11, "For the Son of man is come to **save** *(sozo)* that which was lost."

History shows that through His blood on the cross, Jesus brought *sozo*.

Matthew 27:40, 42, 49, "And saying, Thou that destroy the temple, and build it in three days, **save** *(sozo)* Thyself. If Thou be the Son of God, come down from the cross ... He **saved** *(sozo)* others; Himself He cannot save. If He be the King of Israel, let Him now come down from the cross, and we will believe Him ... The rest said, Let be, let us see whether Elias will come to **save** *(sozo)* Him."

Mark 3:4 (and Luke 6:9), "And He saith unto them, is it lawful to do good on the sabbath days, or to do evil? to **save** *(sozo)* life, or to kill? But they held their peace."

Keep in mind, God and His Word have not changed.

Mark 8:35 (and Luke 17:33), "For whosoever will **save** *(sozo)* his life **shall lose** it; but whosoever shall lose his life for My sake and the Gospel's, the same shall **save** *(sozo)* it." (In this passage, the Greek word for the phrase "shall lose" is *apollumi*, which is co-equally rendered *destroy, to perish*.)

When we destroy our own efforts to obtain *sozo* and simply yield and surrender to God's grace, we then receive *sozo*.

A person must realize that receiving *sozo* is accomplished from a divine, spiritual perspective (way), as God is a Spirit, not an intellect or a physical being.

Mark 16:16, "He that believeth and is baptized shall be **saved** *(sozo);* but he that believeth not shall be damned."

As you study Hebrews 6, you will find that the Bible teaches us about the fundamental doctrines of Christ. In verse 2, there is the doctrine of baptisms. There are three baptisms as you study the Scriptures:

The most important baptism is to be baptized into the body of Christ. This happens when a person is born-again. Then, they are saturated in the body of Christ. Mark 16:16 is talking about this doctrine. When a person is baptized into the body of Christ, they are taking the first step into receiving *sozo*.

The second baptism is the Baptism of the Holy Spirit. When a person receives this baptism, they speak in tongues, God's Heavenly language (see Acts 2:4).

The third baptism is the water baptism.

Sozo becomes a natural reality, when a person believes. It is then that they are submerged into the body of Christ by being born-again.

Luke 7:50, "And He said to the woman, Thy faith hath **saved** *(sozo)* thee; go in peace."

Jesus never touched her or even prayed for her. It was the woman's corresponding actions to God's Word that allowed *sozo* to become a natural reality in her life. She simply received what was already given to her.

Luke 8:12, "Those by the way side are they that hear; then cometh the devil, and taketh away the Word out of their hearts, lest they should believe and be **saved** *(sozo)*."

Luke 9:56, "For the Son of man is not come to destroy men's lives, but to **save** *(sozo)* them. And they went to another village."

Luke 18: 26-27, "And they that heard it said, Who then can be **saved** *(sozo)*? And He said, the things which are impossible with men are possible with God."

Luke 18:35, 41-43, "And it came to pass, that as He was come nigh unto Jericho, a certain blind man sat by the way side begging ... Saying, What wilt Thou that I shall do unto Thee? And he said, Lord, that I may receive my sight. And Jesus said unto him, Receive thy sight: thy faith hath **saved** *(sozo)* thee. And immediately he received his sight, and followed Him, glorifying God: and all the people, when they saw it, gave praise unto God."

Luke 19:10, "For the Son of man is come to seek and to **save** *(sozo)* that which was lost."

Luke 23:35, 37, 39, "And the people stood beholding. And the rulers also with them derided Him, saying, He **saved** *(sozo)* others; let Him save Himself, if He be Christ, the chosen of God ... And saying, If Thou be the King of the Jews, **save** *(sozo)* Thyself ... And one of the malefactors which were hanged railed on Him, saying, If Thou be Christ, **save** *(sozo)* Thyself and us."

These verses shed light on how even the people of Jesus' day knew that He had brought *sozo* to many others. Now, they were challenging Him to establish it in His own life; however, that was not God's plan. The problem with their request was that Jesus came to serve, not to be served (see Matthew 20:28 and Mark 10:45, where the words "minister" and "ministered" are the same Greek word co-equally rendered *serve, servant.* I wonder how many "ministries" throughout the world are serving, as opposed to how many think they are called to be served?)

John 3:17, "For God sent not His Son into the world to condemn the world; but that the world through Him might be **saved** *(sozo)*."

John 5:34, "But I receive not testimony from man: but these things I say, that ye might be **saved** *(sozo)*."

John 10:9, "I am the door: by Me if any man enter in, he shall be **saved** *(sozo)*."

Jesus is the door for receiving what has already been given to us.

John 12:47, "And if any man hear My words, and believe not, I judge him not: for I came not to judge the world, but to **save** *(sozo)* the world."

Acts 2:21, "And it shall come to pass, that whosoever **shall call** on the name of the Lord shall be **saved** *(sozo)*." (In this passage, the Greek word for the phrase "shall call" is *epikaleomai*, which is co-equally rendered *to invoke a decision.*)

Acts 2:40, "And with many other words did he testify and exhort, saying, **save** *(sozo)* yourselves from this untoward generation."

Acts 4:12, "Neither is there **salvation** *(sozo)* in any other: for there is none other name under heaven given among men, whereby we must be **saved** *(sozo)*."

Acts 11:14, "Who shall tell thee words, whereby thou and thy entire house shall be **saved** *(sozo)*."

Acts 15:11, "But we believe that through the grace of the Lord Jesus Christ we shall be **saved** *(sozo)*, even as they."

Peter was proclaiming that the Gentiles could have *sozo*, just as the Jews (see verses 7-10). Keep in mind that we, today, are under the same dispensation, so this is true for us, as well.

Acts 16:30-31, "And brought them out, and said, Sirs, what must I do to be **saved** *(sozo)*? And they said, Believe on the Lord Jesus Christ, and thou shalt be **saved** *(sozo)*, and thy house."

Romans 5:9, "Much more then, being now justified by His blood, we shall be **saved** *(sozo)* from wrath through Him."

Because of the blood of Jesus, we now have *sozo*. When He was brutally beaten and hung on the cross, His blood was spilled, paying the price for us to have *sozo*.

Romans 5:10, "For if, when we were enemies, we were reconciled to God by the death of His Son, much more, being reconciled, we shall be **saved** *(sozo)* by His life."

Romans 8:24, "For we are **saved** *(sozo)* by hope: but hope that is seen is not hope: for what a man seeth, why doth he yet hope for?"

If a person has hope of *sozo*, then reads in God's Word the promise of *sozo*, at some point that hope leaves and faith is established. *Sozo* is then manifested.

Romans 10:9, "That if thou shalt confess with thy mouth the Lord Jesus, and shalt believe in thine heart that God hath raised Him from the dead, thou shalt be **saved** *(sozo)*."

Romans 10:13, "For whosoever shall call upon the name of the Lord shall be **saved** *(sozo)*."

Romans 11:14, "If by any means I may provoke to emulation them, which are my flesh, and might **save** *(sozo)* some of them."

The Apostle Paul knew that *sozo* was available to whoever would accept it. He said that it may upset people by telling them the truth about God and His Word, but it may also cause some to receive *sozo*.

I Corinthians 1:18, "For the preaching of the cross is to them that perish foolishness; but unto us which are **saved** *(sozo)* it is the **power** of God." (In this passage, the Greek word for "power" is *dunamis*, which is co-equally rendered *a miracle itself, miraculous power*.)

We, who have *sozo*, experience the miracle-working power of *sozo*. It is like being born into a family that is gifted to sing. You are simply born with the gift of singing. Similarly, when we are born-again, we are born into *sozo* and simply gifted with *dunamis.*

I Corinthians 1:21, "For after that in the wisdom of God the world by wisdom knew not God, it pleased God by the foolishness of preaching to **save** *(sozo)* them that **believe**." (In this passage, the Greek word for "believe" is *pisteuo*, which is co-equally rendered *commit, entrust, assurance.*)

Sozo comes to those that trust and commit to God's Word that is preached and proclaimed.

I Corinthians 9:22, "To the weak became I as weak, that I might gain the weak: I am made all things to all men, that I might by all means **save** *(sozo)* some."

Notice that Paul made sure his personal customs and culture did not hinder anyone from receiving what God had already given them (*sozo*).

I Corinthians 10:33, "Even as I please all men in all things, not seeking mine own profit, but the profit of many, that they may be **saved** *(sozo)*."

The Apostle Paul sacrificed the comforts of this natural world, so that others could know about and receive *sozo*.

I Corinthians 15:2, "By which also ye are **saved** *(sozo)*, if ye keep in memory what I preached unto you, unless ye have believed in vain."

The Apostle Paul draws our attention to the fact that God has given us everything that is *sozo*. However, Paul established the same fact that Jesus talked about in Mark 4:14-15, when satan immediately comes to steal the Word of God that has just been sown in our lives. Paul also gave Timothy advice along these same lines in I Timothy 6:12, when he told him to "fight the good fight of faith". It is a spiritual, mental and physical battle to continue to believe, talk and act like God's Word is true, when contrary circumstances are present. But it is a good fight, because we win in Jesus' name (see Philippians 2:9).

II Corinthians 2:15, "For we are unto God a sweet savor of Christ, in them that are **saved** *(sozo)*, and in them that perish."

Ephesians 2:5, "Even when we were dead in sins, hath quickened us together with Christ (by grace ye are **saved** *(sozo)*)."

In the mind of God, when Jesus paid the price on the cross for us to have *sozo*, it became a fact in the highest order. If we had it then, we most certainly have it, today!

Ephesians 2:8, "For by grace are ye **saved** *(sozo)* through faith; and that not of yourselves: it is the gift of God."

Galatians 5:4, "Christ is become of no effect unto you, whosever of you are justified by the law; ye are fallen from grace."

Sozo is a divine gift from God. If we try to earn it, we will fall from grace. If we fall from grace, we will actually lose our *sozo* (salvation).

II Thessalonians 2:10, "And with all deceivableness of unrighteousness in them that perish; because they received not the love of the truth, that they might be **saved** *(sozo)."* (This is a divine gift from God. If we try to earn it, we will fall from grace.)

Paul was teaching us that unrighteous people can receive *sozo* if they will simply love the truth of God's Word. Of course, they would then repent from their sins, accept Jesus Christ as their Lord and become a born-again Christian (see Romans 10:9-10).

I Thessalonians 2:16, "Forbidding us to speak to the Gentiles that they might be **saved** *(sozo)*."

The Apostle Paul was aware of the opposition of his preaching the Gospel, yet, he also knew that all he had to do was speak the Gospel and people would receive *sozo*.

I Timothy 1:15, "This is a faithful saying, and worthy of all acceptation, that Christ Jesus came into the world to **save** *(sozo)* sinners; of whom I am chief."

Jesus came and settled the fact that sinners who accept *sozo* become saints.

I Timothy 2:3-4, "For this is good and acceptable in the sight of God our Saviour; Who will have all men to be **saved** *(sozo)*, and to come unto the knowledge of the truth."

God's perfect will is His Word, and according to His will (His Word), He wants everyone to have *sozo* (*healing, wholeness, financial prosperity, safety, perseverance, and those missing body parts*) (see II Peter 3:9).

I Timothy 2:15, "Notwithstanding she shall be **saved** *(sozo)* in childbearing, if they **continue** in faith and charity and holiness with sobriety." (In this passage, the Greek word for "continue" is *meno*, which is co-equally rendered *abide, remain.*)

Even a woman giving birth to a child can be free from the pain of childbearing, if she continues in the faith, trusting and having confidence in the God's Word.

I Timothy 4:16, "Take heed unto thyself, and unto the doctrine; continue in them: for in doing this thou shalt both **save** *(sozo)* thyself, and them that hear thee."

The simple doctrine of God's Word into the ears of someone causes *sozo* to come into their life. It has already been given; people simply need to know it and receive it.

II Timothy 1:9, "Who hath **saved** *(sozo)* us, and called us with a holy calling, not according to our works, but according to His own purpose and grace, which was given us in Christ Jesus before the world began."

Some will say, "If God is all powerful, and He says it's mine, then why do I not have it?" Air is ours, too, but if we refuse to accept it or use it, we will die. Many people are dead spiritually, because they refuse to believe what they cannot see or relate to with their senses.

II Timothy 4:18, "And the Lord shall deliver me from every evil work, and will **preserve** (*sozo*) me unto His Heavenly Kingdom: to Whom be glory forever and ever. Amen."

According to God's Word, we are already preserved in *sozo*, if we will believe and receive.

Titus 3:5, "Not by works of righteousness which we have done, but according to His mercy He **saved** *(sozo)* us, by the washing of **regeneration** and renewing of the Holy Ghost." (In this passage, the Greek word for "regeneration" is *paliggenesia*, which is co-equally rendered *spiritual rebirth, specifically Messianic restoration.*)

Jesus knew that He was going to be leaving this earth, and He prayed to the Father that the Holy Ghost would come in His place. When this took place, all of humanity was given the availability to receive this new spiritual rebirth (*sozo*), which had not been available during the Old Testament days (see John 14:16; 26).

Hebrews 7:25, "Wherefore He is able also to **save** *(sozo)* them to the uttermost that come unto God by Him, seeing He ever liveth to make intercession for them."

James 1:21, "Wherefore lay apart all filthiness and superfluity of naughtiness, and receive with meekness the **engrafted** word, which is able to **save** *(sozo)* your souls." (In this passage, the Greek word for "engrafted" is *emphutos*, which is co-equally rendered *implanted, mighty*.)

Everyone who comes to God can receive *sozo*. Keep in mind that God and His Word are the same thing (see John 1:1). Anyone who will put away sinfulness and receive God's Word will have *sozo*. We need to read God's Word because, "My people are destroyed for a lack of knowledge" (Hosea 4:6).

James 2:14, "What doth it profit, my brethren, though a man say he hath faith, and have not **works**? can faith ***save*** *(sozo)* him?" (In this passage, the Greek word for "works" is *ergon*, which is co-equally rendered *by implication, an act.*)

As you continue to read through to verse 20, this Scripture is made even clearer. If we believe that the Bible is true, the Bible says there are actions that are proof of our belief.

For example, forgiveness is a sound doctrine of the Bible, and we forgive with our actions. Tithing is also an action that we do, because we believe that it gives us the opportunity to invest in the greatest investment of all creation. These actions are God's plan for us to receive what He has given us. By reading verses 14-20, one can easily understand that if there are no corresponding actions of what the Bible says, then that person does not have faith, belief or trust in God or His Word. They simply have only mental assent. Our actions (acting like the Bible is true) cause us to receive the *sozo* that has been provided for every human being.

I Peter 4:18, "And if the righteous scarcely be **saved** *(sozo)*, where shall the ungodly and the sinner appear?"

In the mind of God, the righteous have *sozo*.

James 5:15, "And the prayer of faith shall **save** *(sozo)* the sick, and the Lord shall raise him up; and if he have committed sins, they shall be forgiven him."

True Bible prayer is communicating with God through God's Word. For example, if a person is sick, a Scriptural prayer would be, "I thank You, God, that I Peter 2:24 is true, and I receive my healing now." And they may perceive the Lord saying in return, "Heaven and earth will pass away, but My words will never pass away. And because you know the truth and continue in My truth, the truth will set you free" (see Matthew 24:35; John 8:31-32).

James 5:20, "Let him know, that he which converts the sinner from the error of his way shall **save** *(sozo)* a soul from death, and shall hide a multitude of sins."

When we accept the Good News of salvation, we are accepting and receiving the *sozo* that was given to us from the Lord 2,000 years ago.

I Peter 3:21, "The like figure whereunto even baptism doth also now **save** *(sozo)* us (not the putting away of the filth of the flesh, but the answer of a good conscience toward God) by the resurrection of Jesus Christ."

Instantly, when a person is born-again, they are baptized into the body of Christ, and they begin receiving *sozo.*

(whole)

Matthew 9:21, "For she said within herself, if I may but touch His garment, I shall be **whole** *(sozo).*"

Later in this book, we will study this story in reference to the action she took, but for now we learn that Jesus never actually prayed for this woman. He simply acknowledged that her faith (trust and belief in God) had made her whole. Trust, belief and faith are synonymous terms in the original language of the Holy Scriptures.

Matthew 9:22, "But Jesus turned him about, and when He saw her, He said, Daughter, be of good comfort; thy **faith** hath made thee **whole** *(sozo).* And the woman was made **whole** *(sozo)* from that hour." (In this passage, the Greek word for "faith" is *pistis,* which is co-equally rendered *assurance, belief, confidence, trust, yield.*)

Mark 5:23, "And besought Him greatly, saying, my little daughter lieth at the point of death: I pray Thee, come and lay Thy hands on her, that she may be healed; and she shall **live** *(sozo).*"

Jesus went to Jairus' house; however, by the time Jesus got there, the daughter had died, so Jesus raised her from the dead (see verses 39-42). Jesus gave the request for *sozo*. He raised her from the dead. God has not changed. His *sozo* is still available to all who will receive it.

Mark 5:28, "For she said, If I may touch but His clothes, I shall be **whole** (*sozo*)."

Mark 5:34, "And He said unto her, Daughter, thy faith hath made thee **whole** (*sozo*); go in peace, and be whole of thy plague."

By her efforts, she received a miracle, wholeness and deliverance from an incurable blood disease.

Mark 6:56, "And whithersoever He entered, into villages, or cities, or country, they laid the sick in the streets, and besought Him that they might touch if it were but the border of His garment: and as many as touched Him were made **whole** *(sozo)*."

Mark 10:52, "And Jesus said unto him, Go thy way; thy faith hath made thee **whole** *(sozo)*. And immediately he received his sight, and followed Jesus in the way."

Jesus said that hearing, then believing causes *sozo*. Keep in mind, real Bible faith has expectancy and actions.

Luke 8:36, "They also which saw it told them by what means he that was possessed of the devils was **healed** (*sozo*)."

Luke 8:48, "And He said unto her, Daughter, be of good comfort: thy faith hath made thee **whole** *(sozo)*; go in peace."

Luke 8:50, "But when Jesus heard it, He answered him, saying, Fear not: believe only, and she shall be made **whole** *(sozo)*."

The people received what was already theirs. The *sozo* power was available in the life of Jesus at all times. All a person had to do was to touch Him to receive it. Jesus died on the cross and paid the price for us to simply touch (take, receive) His Word and become whole.

Luke 17:13 tells of ten lepers who asked Jesus to have mercy on them. Jesus said only, "Go show yourselves unto the priests." He knew that the custom of that day was such that if a leper were to ever be cleansed, they would have to validate it by showing themselves to the High Priest.

In verse 14, the Bible says that they were cleansed as they went. Notice, Jesus never preached to them, He never prayed for them, He never touched them. It was their actions with expectancy that made them whole.

Luke 17:19, "And He said unto him, Arise, go thy way: thy faith hath made thee **whole** *(sozo)*."

Jesus acknowledged that the leper's actions made him whole. His actions allowed him to have *sozo*!

Acts 4:9, "If we this day be examined of the good deed done to the impotent man, by what means he is made **whole** *(sozo)*."

Acts 14:8-10, "And there sat a certain man at Lystra, impotent in his feet, being a cripple from his mother's womb, who never had walked: the same heard Paul speak: who steadfastly beholding him, and perceiving that he had faith to be **healed** *(sozo)*. Said with a loud voice, Stand upright on thy feet. And he leaped and walked."

This man simply acted like God's Word was true and received what God had already given him. Again, true Bible belief has expectancy and actions, which activates God's power, His blessings and His promises that have already been given to us.

THE STUDY OF SOTERIA

Now let us look at the word *soteria*. In the Greek, the fuller meaning of this word is *deliver, health, salvation, save, or protect, heal, do well, make whole. Soteria* gets its meaning from its root word *sozo*.

Luke 1:69, “And hath raised up a horn of **salvation** (*soteria*) for us in the house of his servant David.”

We have *soteria*, now, because Jesus came and was raised up.

Luke 1:71, “That we should be **saved** (*soteria*) from our enemies, and from the hand of all that hate us.”

Luke 1:77, “To give knowledge of **salvation** (*soteria*) unto His people by the remission of their sins.”

Jesus brought the knowledge of *soteria*, and we have it in written form, which is the Word of God.

Luke 19:9, “And Jesus said unto him, This day is **salvation** (*soteria*) come to this house...”

Acts 4:12, “Neither is there **salvation** (*soteria*) in any other: for there is none other name under heaven given among men, whereby we must be **saved** (*soteria*).”

We have *soteria*, because we have the name of Jesus (see Philippians 2:9).

Acts 13:26, “Men and brethren, children of the stock of Abraham, and whosoever among **you feareth** God, to you is the word of this **salvation** (*soteria*) sent.” (In this passage, the Greek word for the phrase “you feareth” is *phobeo*, which is co-equally rendered *reverence*.)

Everyone who reverences God can receive *soteria*.

Acts 13:47, "For so hath the Lord commanded us, saying, I have set thee to be a light of the Gentiles, that thou should be for ***salvation*** (*soteria*) unto the ends of the earth."

The ends of the earth have salvation available, now!

Acts 16:17, "The same followed Paul and us, and cried, saying, These men are the servants of the most high God, which show unto us the way of **salvation** (*soteria*)."

Acts 27:34, "Wherefore, I pray you to take some meat: for this is for your **health** (*soteria*): for there shall not a hair fall from the head of any of you."

Romans 1:16, "I am not ashamed of the Gospel (the Word of God) of Christ: for It is power (*dunamis*) of God unto **salvation** (*soteria*) to everyone that believeth" (see Matthew 4:23).

God's power is His Word, and according to His Word, we now have everything that is *sozo*! All we have to do is receive it.

Romans 10:1, "Brethren, my heart's desire and prayer to God for Israel is that they might be **saved** (*soteria*). "

Romans 10:10, "For with the heart man believeth unto righteousness; and with the mouth confession is made unto **salvation** (*soteria*)."

Believing with your heart and confessing with your mouth is how we receive *soteria.*

Romans 11:11, "I say then, Have they stumbled that they should fall? God forbid: but rather through their fall, **salvation** (*soteria*) is come unto the Gentiles."

Romans 13:11, "And that, knowing the time, that now it is high time to awake out of sleep: for now is our **salvation** nearer than when we believed."

The Apostle Paul was trying to stir the people to wake up and receive *soteria*.

II Corinthians 1:6, "And whether we be afflicted, it is for your consolation and **salvation** (*soteria*), which is effectual in the enduring of the same sufferings which we also suffer: or whether we be comforted, it is for your consolation and **salvation** (*soteria*)."

II Corinthians 6:2, "For he saith, I have heard thee in a time accepted, and in the day of **salvation** (*soteria*) have I **succored** thee: behold, now is the accepted time; behold, now is the day of **salvation** (*soteria*)." (In this passage, the Greek word for "succored" is co-equally rendered *help*.)

II Corinthians 7:10, "For Godly sorrow worketh repentance to **salvation** (*soteria*) not to be repented of: but the sorrow of the world worketh death."

Often times, repentance causes *soteria*.

Ephesians 1:13, "In Whom ye also trusted, after that ye heard the word of truth, the Gospel of your **salvation** (*soteria*): in Whom also after that ye believed, ye were sealed with that Holy Spirit of promise."

The Gospel, the Good News of God's Word, causes *soteria*.

Philippians 1:19, "For I know that this shall turn to my **salvation** (*soteria*) through your prayer, and the supply of the Spirit of Jesus Christ."

Philippians 1:28, "And in nothing terrified by your adversaries: which is to them an evident token of perdition, but to you of **salvation** (*soteria*), and that of God."

This verse is talking about the Gospel being preached, so that people can have *soteria* (see verse 27).

Philippians 2:12, "Wherefore, my beloved, as ye have always obeyed, not as in my presence only, but now much more in my absence, **work** out your own **salvation** (*soteria*) with fear and trembling." (In this passage, the Greek word for "work" is *katergazomai*, which is co-equally rendered *accomplish.*)

Soteria is accomplished in a person's life by having great reverence.

I Thessalonians 5:8, "But let us, who are of the day, be sober, putting on the breastplate of faith and love; and for a helmet, the hope of **salvation** (*soteria*)."

We keep *soteria* in our lives by keeping our mind protected with God's Word. Just as a helmet protects the head (the brain), we keep our brain protected (our soul saved) by guarding it with God's Word (see Philippians 4:7-8; Isaiah 26:3). Many new Christians fall back into their old lifestyles, because after they are born-again, they do not get their souls saved. They do not renew or protect their minds with the Word of God.

I Thessalonians 5:9, "For God hath not appointed us to wrath, **but to obtain salvation** (*soteria*) by our Lord Jesus Christ. (In this passage, the Greek word for the phrase "but to obtain" is *peripoiesis,* which is co-equally rendered *purchased, obtained.*)

God purchased and obtained *soteria* for us!

II Thessalonians 2:13, "But we are bound to give thanks always to God for you, brethren beloved of the Lord, because God hath from the beginning chosen you to **salvation** (*soteria*) through sanctification of the Spirit and belief of the truth."

God chose for us to have *soteria* from the very beginning. Keep in mind that God is no respecter of persons; He loves everyone equally.

II Timothy 2:10, "Therefore I endure all things for the elect's sakes, that they may also obtain the **salvation** (*soteria*) which is in Christ Jesus with eternal glory."

II Timothy 3:15, "And that from a child thou hast known the Holy Scriptures, which are able to make thee wise unto **salvation** (*soteria*) through faith which is in Christ Jesus."

How powerful and undeniable that the Holy Scriptures make wise those who experience God's *soteria*!

Hebrews 1:14, "Are they not all ministering spirits, sent forth to minister for them who shall be heirs of **salvation** (*soteria*)?"

God sends His angels to serve and minister to those who are born-again Christians.

Hebrews 2:3, "How shall we escape, if we neglect so great **salvation** (*soteria*); which at the first began to be spoken by the Lord, and was confirmed unto us by them that heard Him."

We will not have a rapture, if we neglect the *soteria* that God has given to the whole human race (see my book entitled, Neglecting Signs & Wonders Is Neglecting The Rapture).

When we know that God has already provided *soteria,* and that it is His divine and perfect will for us to have it, we will have more confidence to believe and receive *soteria*.

Hebrews 2:10, "For it became Him, for Whom are all things, and by Whom are all things, in bringing many sons unto glory, to make the captain of their **salvation** (*soteria*) perfect through sufferings."

Hebrews 5:9, "And being made perfect, He became the author of eternal **salvation** (*soteria*) unto all them that obey Him."

We receive *soteria* when we obey the Scriptures.

Hebrews 6:9, "But, beloved, we are persuaded better things of you, and things that accompany **salvation** (*soteria*), though we thus speak."

Hebrews 9:28, "So Christ was once offered to bear the sins of many; and unto them that look for Him shall

He appear the second time without sin unto **salvation** *(soteria)*."

When the rapture takes place, people out of every kindred, every tongue and every nation will be enjoying *soteria* (see Revelation 5:9, keeping in mind, the rapture does not take place until Revelation 6:1).

I Peter 1:5, "Who are kept by the power of God through faith unto **salvation** *(soteria)* ready to be revealed in the last time."

There is a special *soteria* that God is reserving for the last days (see my book entitled, Neglecting Signs & Wonders Is Neglecting The Rapture).

I Peter 1:9-10, "Receiving the end of your faith, even the **salvation** *(soteria)* of your souls. Of which **salvation** *(soteria)* the prophets have inquired and searched diligently, who prophesied of the grace that should come unto you."

When you read through to verse 12, you will see that there is a salvation that even the prophets of old knew was coming. The angels of Heaven knew about it, and both the angels and the prophets longed to be a part of it, but it is only for this dispensation.

II Peter 3:15, "And account that the longsuffering of our Lord is **salvation** *(soteria)*; even as our beloved brother Paul also according to the wisdom given unto him hath written unto you."

Jude 1:3, "Beloved, when I gave all diligence to write unto you of the common **salvation** *(soteria)*, it was needful for me to write unto you and exhort you that ye should earnestly contend for the faith which was once delivered unto the saints."

In the days of Jude, having *soteria* was a common thing. Keep in mind that we are of that same dispensation.

Revelation 7:10, "And cried with a loud voice, saying, **Salvation** *(soteria)* to our God which sitteth upon the throne, and unto the Lamb."

If Jesus Christ is our Lord and Savior, then everything that belongs to God has been given to us (see I Corinthians 6:19).

Revelation 12:10, "And I heard a loud voice saying in Heaven, Now is come **salvation** *(soteria)*, and strength, and the Kingdom of our God, and the power of his Christ..."

Revelation 19:1, "And after these things I heard a great voice of much people in Heaven, saying, Alleluia; **Salvation** *(soteria)*, and glory, and honor, and power, unto the Lord our God."

CHAPTER 3

AITOE

There are 68 verses in the New Testament that use the Greek word *aitoe,* which means *ask, desire, crave, require; to strictly demand of something due*. This chapter looks at the prominent New Testament verses that use the word *aitoe* to support our rights to strictly demand that satan give back what he has stolen from us, when the promise of God's Word states that it is ours.

Matthew 6:8, "Be not ye therefore like unto them: for your Father knoweth what things ye have need of, before ye **ask** *(aitoe)* **Him**." (The word "Him" used at the end of this verse is your self in the Greek manuscripts.)

In reading verse 7, you will notice that Jesus is telling us to not be like the heathen who use vain repetitions; thinking if they cry and beg long enough,

God will do something for them. Instead, in the next verse, Jesus tells us how we should pray, "Strictly demand satan to give back what has been stolen!"

In verse 10, Jesus tells us that we need to demand that it be on earth as it is in Heaven! So many Christians have lived defeated lives, begging, fasting and praying for God to do something that He has already done, as I'm sure the devil sits back and laughs. If we want what God's Word says is ours, we must get militant with the devil!

Matthew 7:7-8, "**Ask** *(aitoe)*, and it shall be given you; seek, and ye shall find; knock, and it shall be opened unto you. For every one that **asketh** *(aitoe)* receiveth; and he that seeketh findeth; and to him that knocketh it shall be opened."

In these two verses, it is very obvious why people do not have. They do not *aiteo*!

Matthew 7:9-11, "Or what man is there of you, whom if his son **ask** *(aitoe)* bread, will he give him a stone?" Or if he **ask** *(aitoe)* a fish, will he give him a serpent? If ye then, being evil, know how to give **good** gifts unto your children, how much more shall your Father which is in Heaven give **good things to them** that **ask** *(aitoe)* Him? (In this passage, the Greek word for "good" is *didomi*, which is co-equally rendered *power*. The phrase "things to them" is not in the Greek at all.)

So, accurately translated, the last portion of this verse would be, "...your Father which is in Heaven has power for those that strictly demand satan to give what is due them."

Matthew 18:19, "Again I say unto you, That if two of you shall agree on earth as touching anything that they shall **ask** *(aitoe)*, it shall be done for them of My Father which is in Heaven."

The Lord is telling us that if we strictly demand what is ours, IT SHALL BE DONE, and the Father will make sure of it.

Matthew 21:22, "And all things, whatsoever ye shall **ask** *(aitoe)* in prayer, believing, ye shall receive."

Can Jesus be any clearer?

Mark 11:24, "Therefore I say unto you, What things soever ye **desire** (*aitoe*), when ye pray, believe that ye receive them, and ye shall have them."

As Brother Hagin would say, "This is the golden text of faith in the Bible." I would have to agree that this is the strongest verse in the Bible for the believer.

Luke 11:9, “And I say unto you, **Ask** *(aitoe)*, and it shall be given you; seek, and ye shall find; knock, and it shall be opened unto you.”

There is not a stronger English assertion than, “it shall be given you.”

Luke 11:10-11, “For every one that **asketh** *(aitoe)* receiveth; and he that seeketh findeth; and to him that knocketh it shall be opened. If a son shall **ask** *(aitoe)* bread of any of you that is a father, will he give him a stone? Or if he ask a fish, will he for a fish give him a serpent?”

God watches over His Word that is alive in our lives to make sure we do not get a counterfeit.

Luke 11:12-13, “Or if he shall **ask** *(aitoe)* an egg, will he offer him a scorpion? If **ye then**, being evil, know how to **give** good gifts unto your children: how much more shall your Heavenly Father **give** the Holy Spirit to them that **ask** *(aitoe)* him?” (In this passage, the Greek word for the phrase “ye then” is *oun,* which is co-equally rendered *certainly, truly*. Also, the Greek word for “give” is *didomi*, which is co-equally rendered *grant*.)

There is a very loving way that we are actually demanding from God at times; not unlike a baby would reach out their arms for their mother, in both a demanding yet loving and dependant way. Of course, a mother loves this kind of a gentle, loving demand. How much more does our Father God love it when we let Him know that we cannot live without Him and that we need Him?

John 4:10, "Jesus answered and said unto her, If thou knewest the gift of God, and Who it is that saith to thee, Give Me to drink; thou wouldest have **asked** *(aitoe)* of Him, and He would have given thee living water."

Jesus tells us that because of the price He paid, we can have divine life, if we will strictly demand what is due us.

John 11:22, "But I know, that even now, whatsoever thou wilt **ask** *(aitoe)* of God, God will give it thee."

John 12:13-14 (and John 16:23), "And whatsoever ye shall **ask** *(aitoe)* in My name, that will I do, that the Father may be glorified in the Son. If ye shall **ask** *(aitoe)* anything in My name, I will do it."

John 14:12-13, "Verily, verily, I say unto you, He that believeth on Me, that works that I do shall he do also; and greater works than these shall he do; because I go unto My Father. And whatsoever ye shall **ask** *(aitoe)* in My name, that will I do, that the Father maybe glorified in the Son."

John 14:14, "If ye shall **ask** *(aitoe)* any thing in My name, I will do it."

On more than one occasion, I've heard Brother Kenneth Hagin explain John 14:14 by quoting Dr. P.C. Nelson. In the 1950's, a popular magazine described Dr. P.C. Nelson as the leading authority of his day in the Greek language and second-ranked authority in the Hebrew language. He could read and write 32 languages and was the founder of Southwestern Bible School in Enid, Oklahoma. Dr. P.C. Nelson translated this verse more accurately to say, "If you ask anything in My name, if it does not exist, I will make it for you."

Apostle Gary Meador, the president and founder of Rhema Bible College in Costa Rica, was my interpreter at a crusade I was holding in Chinadega, Nicaragua in 2000. During this crusade, I asked those who were completely blind and wanted to instantly receive their sight by God's recreating power to join me on the platform. A tearful mother brought her 8 year-old daughter up to the stage. The girl was born with no eyes. As the power of God went into that little girl's face, two beautiful brown eyes were created. As this happened, I recalled Dr. P.C. Nelson's translation, "If you ask anything in My name, if it does not exist I will make it for you."

John 15:7, "If ye abide in Me, and My words abide in you, ye shall **ask** *(aitoe)* what ye will, and it shall be done unto you."

John 15:16, "Ye have not chosen Me, but I have chosen you, and ordained you, that ye should go and bring forth fruit, and that your fruit should remain: that whatsoever ye shall **ask** *(aitoe)* of the Father in My name, He may give it you."

Notice the clear order of true Scriptural prayer: ask the Father in Jesus' name and then He will give it you. We should not be praying to Jesus, any more than someone should pray to Mary. In order to be Scripturally sound, we are to pray to the Father in the name of Jesus.

John 16:24, "Hitherto have ye **asked** *(aitoe)* nothing in My name: **ask** *(aitoe)*, and ye shall receive, that your joy may be full."

John 16:26, "At that day ye shall **ask** *(aitoe)* in My name: and I say not unto you, that I will pray the Father for you."

Luke 11:10, "For everyone that **asketh** *(aitoe)* receiveth."

Acts 3:2, "And a certain man lame from his mother's womb was carried, whom they laid daily at the gate of the temple which is called Beautiful, to **ask** *(aitoe)* alms of them that entered into the temple."

If you read this entire story, you will find in Acts 3:1-7, this man was crippled from birth and was now over forty years of age (see Acts 4:22). In reading the Gospels (Matthew, Mark, Luke and John), you will find that Jesus went into this Temple many times, but had never prayed for this man who lay daily at its entrance.

We know from the Scriptures that Jesus had the perfect mind of God and that God wants everyone to receive *sozo* (see II Peter 3:9), yet He did not pray for him. Even though he must have heard many of Jesus' teachings in that temple (the best sermons and teachings ever ministered on earth!), he did not yet have the faith or expectancy to receive (see Mark 6:5-6).

However, in Acts 3:5, Peter saw that the man had changed. Peter walked by this man at the gate of temple, and the man was now asking, craving, requiring and demanding what is due him, "He gave heed unto them, EXPECTING to receive."

Acts 5:9, "The same heard Paul speak: who steadfastly beholding him, and perceiving that he had faith to be **healed** (*sozo*)."

He expected to receive, and then he was made **whole** (*sozo*) (see Acts 4:9).

Peter did not have more compassion or power than did Jesus, and God did not change. The man changed. He was now demanding what was due, with great anticipation of receiving.

Mark 6:5 describes a similar condition with the entire city of Nazareth, "He could there do no mighty work, save that He laid His hands upon a few sick folk, and healed them."

The Bible does not say, "He would not", It says, "He could not." The reason followed in verse 6, "He marveled because of their unbelief." Real Bible belief has expectancy and actions of demanding what is due, actions of determination.

Ephesians 3:20, "Now unto Him that is able to do exceeding abundantly above all that we **ask** *(aitoe)* or think, according to the power that **worketh** in us." (In this passage, the Greek word for "worketh" is *energeo*, which is co-equally rendered *to be active*.)

If we want to see the power of God's Word as a natural reality in our lives, we must have spiritual, mental and physical actions.

Colossians 1:9, "For this cause we also, since the day we heard it, do not cease to pray for you, and to **desire** (*aiteo*) that ye might be filled with the knowledge of His will in all wisdom and spiritual understanding."

Paul was demanding for others what was due them. This verse correlates with Galatians 4:19, "I travail in birth again until Christ be formed in you." If we want to see lives change, this is a perfect, powerful God-ordained prayer and warfare.

James 1:5, "If any of you lack wisdom, let him **ask** *(aitoe)* of God, that giveth to all men liberally, and upbraideth not; and it shall be given him."

If we lack the wisdom that God has already given us, all we have to do is crave, require, and strictly demand it, as it is due us.

James 1:6-8, "But let him **ask** *(aitoe)* in faith, nothing wavering. For he that wavereth is like a wave of the sea driven with the wind and tossed. For let not that man think that he shall receive any thing of the Lord. A double-minded man is unstable in all his ways."

James 4:2, "...ye have not because ye **ask** *(aitoe)* not."

God has already given us everything we could possibly need or desire in this life. So, if we do not possess those things, it is quite possibly due to the fact that we are not strictly demanding (with our spirits, minds and natural actions) what is due. For when we finally do this, we are demanding satan and circumstances to return what has been stolen from us.

Many Christians have been defeated in this area, because the devil may say to them, "you are asking amiss to consume it to your lust." However, if you are asking in agreement with God's Word, then you are asking (demanding due) what God's Word has promised you!

I John 5:14, "And this is the confidence that we have in Him, that, if we **ask** *(aitoe)* anything according to His will, He heareth us."

Supernatural, divine confidence comes when our asking is in agreement with God's Word (God's will).

I John 5:15, "And if we know that He hear us, whatsoever we **ask** *(aitoe)*, we know that we have the petitions that we **desired** (*aitoe*) of Him."

I John 5:16, "If any man see his brother sin a sin which is not unto death, he shall **ask** *(aitoe)*, and He shall give him life for them that sin not unto death. There is a sin unto death: I do not say that he shall pray for it."

This is the power of the word *aitoe*. We can actually ask God to forgive people of their sin, and He will (with the exception of those who reject Jesus Christ as their Lord and blaspheme the Holy Spirit). This prayer needs to be in our life on a daily basis, especially for our loved ones.

When people sin, it gives satan the right to blind their eyes, keeping them from the light of God's great blessings (see II Corinthians 4:3-7). So, when we destroy those evil influences, our loved ones can then be influenced by the voice of the Holy Spirit.

I John 3:22, "And whatsoever we **ask** *(aitoe)*, we receive of Him, because we keep His commandments, and do those things that are pleasing in His sight."

CHAPTER 4

BECAUSE OF CHRIST

There are approximately 144 verses in the New Testament that use the following expressions:

by His blood
with Him, with Christ
by Him, by Christ, by Me
in Him, in Christ, in Me
in My name
of Him, of Himself
in My love
by Whom, from Whom, in Whom
in the Beloved, in the Lord
through Christ, through Him, through the Word

These passages use different phrasings, yet teach the same message that God has already given us all things that pertain to this life and Godliness (God-likeness) in this natural and spiritual life.

When Jesus died on the cross, He paid the price that we would be in Him (in Christ/with Him). In essence, Jesus paid the price that everything He has would be given to us.

BY HIS BLOOD

Hebrews 9:11-12, "...**by His blood** He entered in once into the holy place, having obtained eternal redemption for us."

Jesus paid the price so we would be redeemed from poverty, sickness and death. As you study this, you will find that it is both physical and spiritual, as God Himself, experiences.

Hebrews 9:14-15, "How much more shall the **blood of Christ**, Who through the eternal Spirit offered Himself without spot to God, purge your conscience from dead works to serve the living God? And for this cause He is mediator of the New Testament, that by means of death, for the redemption of the transgressions that were under the first testament, they which are **called** might receive the promise of eternal inheritance." (In this passage, the Greek word for "called" is *kaleō,* which is co-equally rendered *to call aloud.*)

As seen in II Peter 3:9, it is God's will that every person has eternal life, "The Lord ... is longsuffering to us-ward, not willing that any should perish, but that all should come to repentance (change)."

Translated from the Greek, this passage would be more accurately said, "...they which call aloud to all might receive the promise of eternal inheritance, because of the blood of Jesus Christ."

I John 1:7, "But if we walk in the **light** as He is in the **light**, we have fellowship one with another, and the **blood of Jesus Christ** His Son cleanseth us from all sin." (In this passage, the Greek word for "light" is *phōs*, which is co-equally rendered *to shine or make manifest, especially by rays, luminousness, fire, light.*)

The blood of Jesus not only cleanses us from all sins, but it has also paid the price for us to walk in the supernatural light, which is God's glory. His Glory causes supernatural rays of luminousness fire (light) to go from us, causing manifestations of miracles in our lives and in the lives of others.

WITH HIM/ WITH CHRIST

Romans 6:4, "Therefore we are buried **with Him** ...so we also should walk in newness of life (*zoe*)!"

Romans 6:6, "Knowing this, that our old man is crucified **with Him**, that the body of sin might be destroyed, that henceforth we should not serve sin."

When Jesus died on the cross, He paid the price so that when we accept Him as our Lord, the longing (the bondage of the sin nature) would be broken off of us.

Romans 6:8, "Now if we be dead with Christ, we believe that we shall also live **with Him**."

Romans 8:32, "He (God) that spared not His own Son, but delivered Him up for us all, how shall He not **with Him** also freely give us all things."

Most people believe the first part of this verse (that God gave His only Son for us); however, most do not believe the last part of the verse, which says that because of the price that God paid, ALL things have been given to us. If the first part of the verse is true, so is the rest!

Colossians 2:13-15, "And you being dead in your sins and the uncircumcision of your flesh, hath He quickened together **with Him**, having forgiven you all trespasses; Blotting out the **handwriting of ordinances** that was against us, which was contrary to us, and took it out of the way, nailing it to His cross; And having spoiled principalities and powers, He made a shew of them openly, triumphing over them in it" (see II

Corinthians 13:4; Colossians 3:3). (In this passage, the Greek word for "handwriting" is *cheirographon*, co-equally rendered *legal power*. The Greek word for "ordinances" is *dogma*, co-equally rendered *law*.)

In the mind of God, Jesus took our place on the cross. So, when victory was won over satan and all of his powers, we were quickened to that co-equal position of victory with Christ. All of the laws of ill will that were against us (sickness, disease, poverty, depression, etc.) were spoiled and rendered useless.

II Timothy 2:11-12, "For if we be dead **with Him**, we shall also live with Him."

Ephesians 2:5, "Even when we were dead in sins, hath quickened us together **with Christ** (by grace ye are saved)."

Jesus paid the price on the cross for us to be quickened together **with Him**. We are what He is, and have what He has (see Romans 6:8; Galatians 2:20; Colossians 2:20, 3:1-3).

BY HIM / BY CHRIST / BY ME

John 14:6, "Jesus saith unto him, I am the way, the truth, and the life: no man cometh unto the Father, but **by Me**."

Keep in mind that Jesus is the Word. If we want more life (*zoe*), all we have to do is believe that the Word is the way and the truth.

Romans 3:22, "Even the righteousness of God which is **by** faith of **Jesus Christ** unto all and upon all them that believe: for there is no difference."

We have the righteousness of God by our faith, trust and belief in Jesus Christ.

Romans 5:15, "For if through the offence of one (Adam) many be dead (spiritually), much more the grace of God, and the gift by grace, which is **by One man, Jesus Christ**, hath abounded unto many. "

Romans 5:17, "For if by one man's offence death reigned by one; much more they which receive abundance of grace and of the gift of righteousness of One the free gift of righteousness shall reign in life **by One, Jesus Christ**."

We have the free gift of righteousness because of Jesus.

Romans 5:18, "Therefore as by the offence of one judgment came upon all men to condemnation; even so by the righteousness of One the free gift came upon all men unto justification of life."

The power and influence of Jesus is much more than that of Adam. And by His power, all people are justified and declared innocent in every area of thinking. All they need to do is believe, accept and receive it.

I Corinthians 1:5, "That in EVERYTHING, ye are enriched **by Him**, in all utterance, and in all knowledge."

II Corinthians 5:18, "...God hath **reconciled** us to Himself **by Jesus Christ**..." (In this passage, the Greek word for "reconciled" is *katallassō*, co-equally rendered *to change mutually, to compound a difference*.)

Galatians 2:16, "...we have believed in Jesus Christ, that we might be **justified by** the faith of **Christ**, and not by the works of the law." (In this passage, the Greek word for "justified" is *dikaioō*, co-equally rendered *innocent, be righteous, holy*.)

Ephesians 1:5, "...we have been adopted as children of God **by Jesus Christ**."

Philippians 1:11, "Being filled with the fruits of righteousness, which are **by Jesus Christ**, unto the glory and praise of God."

Philippians 4:19, "But my God shall supply all your **need** according to His riches in glory **by Christ Jesus**. (In this passage, the Greek word for "need" is *chreia*, co-equally rendered *lack, necessary, want*.)

Keep in mind, God is such a good God, that He has already met your needs AND your wants by Jesus Christ.

Hebrews 1:3, "...**by Himself** purged our sins."

Jesus washed away our sins.

I Peter 2:5, "Ye are ... a holy priesthood ... acceptable to God **by Jesus Christ**."

I Peter 5:10, "But the God of all grace, Who hath called us unto His eternal **glory by Christ Jesus** ... " (In this passage, the Greek word for "glory" is *doxa*, co-equally rendered *God's reputation.*)

Because of price that Jesus paid, we now have the reputation of God (see Romans 7:4; I Corinthians 1:1-3).

IN HIM / IN CHRIST / IN ME

John 1:4, "**In Him** was life; and the life was **the light** of men." (In this passage, the Greek word for the phrase "the light" is *phōs,* co-equally rendered *to shine or make manifest, especially by rays; fire, light.*)

As we abide in Christ, we have the miracle-working power of God that shines from us in the form of rays of light to make manifest God's Miracles from the divine spirit world into the natural world (see John 3:15-16).

John 6:56, "He that eateth My **flesh**, and drinketh **My blood**, dwelleth **in Me**, and I in him. (In this passage, the Greek word for "flesh" is *sarx*, which is co-equally rendered *strictly food*. The phrase "my blood" is *aima*, which is co-equally rendered *the atoning blood of Christ; by implication bloodshed, figuratively*.)

The provision has already been made for living in Christ and in all of the promises of God's Word. All we need to do is to partake of it.

John 14:20, "At that day ye shall know that I am in My Father, and ye **in Me**, and I in you."

John 15:4-5, "Abide **in Me**, and I in you: As the branch cannot bear fruit of itself, except it abide in the vine; no more can ye, except ye abide **in Me**. I am the vine, ye are the branches: he that abideth **in Me**, and I in him, the same bringeth forth much fruit: for without Me ye can do nothing."

God has given us the privilege to abide in Him; the decision is ours.

John 15:7-8, "If ye abide **in Me,** and My words abide in you, ye shall **ask** *(aitoe)* what ye will, and it shall be done unto you. Herein is My Father glorified that ye bear much fruit; so shall ye be My disciples."

John 16:33, "These things I have spoken **unto you, that in Me ye might have peace**." (In this passage, the

Greek word for the phrase "unto you, that in Me ye might have" is *echo,* co-equally rendered *to hold as possession, possessed with, enjoy, necessity.* Also, the Greek word for "peace" is *eirēnē,* which is co-equally rendered *prosperity and rest.*)

God's Word is the key to receiving the divine prosperity and rest that God has already given to us.

Acts 17:28, "... **in Him** ... we are also His offspring ..."

Romans 3:24, "**Being justified** freely by His Grace through the redemption that is **in Christ Jesus**." (In this passage, the Greek word for the phrase "being justified" is *dikaioō,* co-equally rendered *innocent, free, righteous, holy.*)

Romans 8:1-2, "There is therefore now NO condemnation to them which are **in Christ Jesus**, who walk not after the flesh, but after the Spirit. For the law of the Spirit of life **in Christ Jesus** hath made me free from the law of sin and death."

Romans 12:5, "So we, being many, are one body **in Christ**, and every one members one of another."

I Corinthians 1:2, "... to those sanctified **in Christ** Jesus and called to be His holy people, together with all those everywhere who call on the name of our Lord Jesus Christ ..."

I Corinthians 1:30, "But of Him are ye **in Christ Jesus**, who of God is made unto us wisdom, and righteousness, and sanctification, and redemption."

II Corinthians 1:21, "Now He which establisheth us with you **in Christ and hath anointed** us, is God." (In this passage, the Greek word for the phrase "and hath anointed" is *chrio*, co-equally rendered *to give oracles: which is the highest order of recommendation, honor and calling that comes from God*.)

Because of Jesus, we are children of the God of all power!

I Corinthians 8:6, "But to us there is but one God, the Father of whom are all things, and we **in Him** ... " (see Colossians 1:16, 17:20, 3:17; Hebrews 7:25, 13:15; I Peter 1:21)

I Corinthians 15:22, "... even so **in Christ** shall all be made alive."

II Corinthians 1:20, "For all the promises of God **in Him** are yea, and in Him Amen, unto the glory of God by us!"

II Corinthians 2:14, "Now thanks be unto God, which always causeth **us to triumph in Christ**, and maketh manifest the Savior of His knowledge by us in every place." (In this passage, the Greek word for the phrase "us to triumph" is *thriambeuō*, co-equally rendered *to conquer or to give victory*.)

II Corinthians 5:17, "... if any man be **in Christ**, he is a new creature: old things are passed away; behold, all things are become new."

II Corinthians 5:19, "To wit, that God was **in Christ**, **reconciling** the world unto Himself, **not imputing** their trespasses unto them; and hath committed unto us the word of **reconciliation**. (In this passage, the Greek word for "reconciling" is *katallassō*, co-equally rendered *exchange*. The phrase "not imputing" in the Greek is *logizomai*, co-equally rendered *despise, count*. The Greek word for "reconciliation" is *katallage*, co-equally rendered *exchange, to divine favor*.)

In essence, when we are in Christ, God is not counting up our wrongdoings. Instead, He has exchanged the penalty of sin for divine favor!

All of God's promises (which is His Word) come to pass in this natural world, because we are in Christ!

II Corinthians 5:21, "For He hath made Him to be sin for us, Who knew no sin: that we might be made the **righteousness** of God **in Him**." (In this passage, the Greek word for "righteousness" is *dikaiosunē*, co-equally rendered *justification, absolutely innocent, holy*.)

Because we are in Him, we are absolutely innocent of any ill will, and we are holy, as our Father God is holy.

Galatians 3:26, "For ye are all the children of God by faith **in Christ Jesus**" (see Galatians 2:4; 5:6, 28; 6:15).

Ephesians 1:3, " ... the God and Father of our Lord Jesus Christ, Who hath blessed us with all spiritual blessings in Heavenly places **in Christ**" (see verse 10).

Ephesians 1:4, "... He hath chosen us **in Him** before the foundation of the world, that we should be holy and without blame before Him in love."

Ephesians 2:6, "And hath raised us up together, and made us sit together in Heavenly places **in Christ Jesus"** (see Ephesians 2:10, 13; 3:6; Philippians 3:13-14).

Philippians 3:9, "... **in Him**, not having mine own righteousness, which is of the law, but that which is through the faith of Christ, the righteousness which is of God by faith."

Colossians 1:28, " ... teaching every man (person), in all wisdom; that we may present every man perfect **in Christ Jesus**."

Colossians 2:6-7, 10, "And ye are complete **in Him**, which is the head of all principality and power."

I Thessalonians 4:16, "For the Lord Himself shall descend from Heaven with a shout, with the voice of the archangel, and with the trump of God: and the dead **in Christ** shall rise first" (see I Thessalonians 5:18; I Timothy 1:14; II Timothy 1:9, 13; 2:1).

II Timothy 2:10, "Therefore, I endure all things for the elect's sakes, that they may also obtain the salvation which is **in Christ Jesus** with eternal **glory**." (In this passage, the Greek word for "glory" is *doxa*, which is co-equally rendered *the reputation of God*.)

Because we are in Christ, we have the very reputation of God (see II Timothy 3:15).

Philemon 1:6, "That the communication of thy faith may become **effectual** by the acknowledging of every good thing which is in you **in Christ Jesus**." (In this passage, the Greek word for "effectual" is *energēs*, co-equally rendered *active, operative, powerful*.)

When we speak and write to others of the good things, which are in you because you are in Christ, your faith becomes powerful (see II Peter 1:8; II John 1:9).

I John 2:5-6, 8, 27, "But the anointing which **ye have received of Him** abideth in you ... abide **in Him**." (In this passage, the Greek word for the phrase "ye have received" is *lambanō*, which is co-equally rendered *to have offered to one*.)

In the mind of God, His anointing has been offered to us, given to us and abides in us.

I John 2:28, "... abide **in Him** ... may have confidence, and be not ashamed before Him at His coming."

I John 3:3, "And **every man that hath** this **hope in Him purifieth** himself, even as He is pure." (In this passage, the Greek word for "every" is *pas*, which is co-equally rendered *anyone, whosoever*. The phrase, "man that hath" is *echō*, which is co-equally rendered *to hold, possessed with, enjoy, have, keep*. The Greek word for "hope" is *elpis*, which is co-equally rendered *to anticipate, usually with pleasure, expectation*. The Greek word for "purifieth" is *hagnizō*, co-equally rendered *to make clean, innocent, perfect*.)

I John 3:5, "And ye know that He was manifested to take away our sins; and **in Him** is no sin."

I John 3:6, "Whosoever abideth **in Him** sinneth not: whosoever sinneth hath not seen Him, neither known Him."

This is sin of rejecting Jesus Christ as Lord. And when we are in Christ, we no longer have that sin in our lives (see I John 3:24, 4:13).

I John 5:14, "And this is the confidence that we have **in Him**, that if we ask anything according to His will, He heareth us."

In Him, there is a supernatural confidence that when we ask God for something in agreement with His will (His Word), He hears us!

I John 5:15, "And if we know that He hear us, whatsoever we ask, we know that we have the petitions that we desire of Him."

God hearing us is equivalent to God giving us the petition (see verse 20).

IN MY NAME

Matthew 18:20, "For where two or three are gathered together **in My name**, there am I in the midst of them."

God has already provided His presence to be with us at all times. However, we need to take the initiative to get into His presence, by believing God's Word (Hebrews 13:5).

Mark 16:17-18, "And these **signs** shall follow them that believe; **in My name** shall they cast out devils; they shall speak with new tongues; they shall take up serpents; and if they drink any deadly thing, it shall not hurt them: they shall lay hands on the sick, and they shall recover." (In this passage, the Greek word for "signs" is *sēmeion*, which is co-equally rendered *especially supernaturally, miracle, wonder, supernatural* *miracles in the senses realm confirming the atoning work of Christ.*)

John 14:13-14, "And whatsoever ye shall ask **in My name**, that will I do that the Father may be glorified in the Son. If ye shall ask any thing **in My name**, I will do it." (Refer to the previous chapter, when I spoke about Dr. P.C. Nelson's Greek translation, "If you ask any thing IN MY NAME, if it does not exist, I will make it for you!")

John 16:23-24, "And in that day ye shall ask Me nothing. Verily, verily, I say unto you, whatsoever ye shall ask the Father **in My name**, He will give it you. Hitherto have ye asked (*aitoe*) nothing **in My name**: ask, and ye shall receive, that your joy may be full."

The same truth is applied here as in John 14:12-14. It is our privilege and our responsibility to demand satan and circumstances to surrender unto us what belongs to us. God has already has given us everything that pertains to this life and Godliness.

I Corinthians 6:11, "And such were some of you: but ye are **washed**, but ye are **sanctified** but ye are **justified in the name of the Lord Jesus**, and by the Spirit of our God." (In this passage, the Greek word for "washed" is *apolouō*, which is co-equally rendered *complete*. The Greek word for "sanctified" is *hagiazō*, which is co-equally rendered *to make holy, that is, purify* *or be holy.* The Greek word for "justified" is *dikaioō,* which is co-equally rendered *innocent, free, righteous.*)

OF HIM / OF HIMSELF

Hebrews 9:26, "He appeared to put away sin by the sacrifice **of Himself**."

I John 2:27, "**But the anointing** which **ye have received of Him** abideth in you, and ye need not that any man teach you ... the same anointing teacheth you of all things, and is truth ... " (In this passage, the Greek word for the phrase "but the anointing" is *chrisma,* which is co-equally rendered *the special endowment of the Holy Spirit.* The Greek word for the phrase "ye have received" is *lambanō,* which is co-equally rendered *to take, get hold of.*)

IN MY LOVE

John 15:9-11, "As the Father hath loved Me, so have I loved you: continue ye **in My love**. If ye keep My commandments, ye shall abide **in My love**; even as I have kept My Father's commandments, and abide **in His love**. These things have I spoken unto you, that My joy might remain in you, and that your joy might be full."

God has already given us His joy. Nehemiah 8:10 tells us that the joy of the Lord is our strength! When we have God's joy, we have God's strength.

II Samuel 22:33, "God is my strength and power: and He maketh my way perfect!"

If satan can keep you away from God's Word, he will keep you away from God's joy (God's strength).

BY WHOM / FROM WHOM / IN WHOM

Romans 5:2, "**By Whom** also we have access by faith, into this grace wherein we stand, and rejoice in hope of the glory of God."

Because of the price that Jesus paid, we have access to stand and live in God's glory.

Romans 5:11, "...our Lord Jesus Christ, **by Whom** we have now received the **atonement**." (In this passage, the Greek word for "atonement" is *katallagē*, which is co-equally rendered *exchange, restoration to divine favor, reconciliation.*)

We have been restored to God's divine favor, because of Jesus (see Galatians 6:14).

Ephesians 4:16, "**From Whom** the whole body fitly joined together and compacted by that which every joint supplieth, according to the effectual working in the measure of every part, maketh increase of the body unto the edifying of itself in love" (see Colossians 2:19).

Ephesians 1:7, "**In Whom** we have redemption through His blood, the forgiveness of sins, according to the riches of His grace."

We have been redeemed from sickness, disease, poverty, unhappiness and hell. God sent His only Son, Jesus, to pay the price, so that we would be redeemed from the wages of sin and imperfection, as Heaven is too holy and pure for us to ever earn our own way.

Ephesians 1:11, "**In Whom** also we have obtained an inheritance ... "

Jesus paid the price for us to have such a divine inheritance.

Ephesians 2:19-22, "Now therefore ye are no more strangers. **In Whom** all the building fitly framed together groweth unto a holy temple in the Lord: And are built upon the foundation of ... Jesus Christ ... **In Whom** ye also are builded together for a habitation of God through the Spirit."

Ephesians 3:11, "According to the eternal purpose which He purposed in Christ Jesus our Lord."

The same eternal purpose of Christ is now in us. We are now the hope of God's Glory; His reputation being revealed and known in this world (see Ephesians 3:19; Colossians 1:26-27).

Colossians 1:14, "**In Whom** we have redemption through His blood, even the forgiveness of sins."

Redemption and forgiveness is ours, if we receive it. We must fully understand that just because something is given, does not mean it becomes reality until that person receives it.

Colossians 2:3, "In Whom are hid all the treasures of wisdom and knowledge."

If we will receive it, this passage belongs to the entire human race (see Colossians 2:11; I Peter 1:8).

IN THE BELOVED / IN THE LORD

Ephesians 1:6, "To the praise of the glory of His grace, wherein He hath made **us accepted in the Beloved**." (In this passage, the Greek word for the phrase "us accepted" is *charitoō*, which is co-equally rendered *indue with special honor: be highly favored*.)

Because of Christ, we are highly favored and endued with special honor.

Ephesians 5:8, "For ye were sometimes darkness, but now are ye **light in the Lord**: walk as children of **light**." (In this passage, the Greek word for "light" is *phōs,* which is co-equally rendered *to shine or make manifest, especially by rays.*)

God has given us the privilege to walk and live in His supernatural Shekhinah Glory (see Habakkuk 3:3-4, Amplified Bible version)!

Ephesians 6:10, "Finally, my brethren, be strong **in the Lord**, and in the power of His might."

The decision is ours! We must be strong.

THROUGH CHRIST / THROUGH HIM / THROUGH THE WORD

John 3:17, "For God sent not His Son into the world to condemn the world; but that the world **through Him** might be saved."

John 15:3, "Now, **ye are clean through the word** which I have spoken unto you." (In this passage, the Greek word for the phrase "ye are clean" is *katharos,* which is co-equally rendered *pure, blameless, innocent.*)

Romans 5:1, "Therefore **being justified** by faith, we have peace with God **through our Lord Jesus Christ**." (In this passage, the Greek word for the phrase, "being justified" is *dikaioō*, which is co-equally rendered *just or innocent: free, be righteous*. The root word is *dikaios*, meaning *innocent, holy, absolutely just, righteous*.)

Romans 5:9, "Much more then, being now justified by His blood, we shall be saved **from wrath through Him**." (In this passage, the Greek word for the phrase "from wrath" is *orgē*, which is co-equally rendered *punishment, anger, vengeance*.)

Because of Christ, we are saved from satan's punishment and anger!

Romans 5:11, " ... **through our Lord Jesus Christ**, by Whom we have now received the **atonement**." (In this passage the Greek word for "atonement" is *katallagē*, which is co-equally rendered *restoration, divine favor, reconciliation*.)

Romans 6:11, "Likewise reckon ye also yourselves to be dead indeed unto sin, but alive unto God **through Jesus Christ our Lord**."

When we start accepting God's Word, we can be free from the strongholds of sin and made alive unto God.

Romans 6:23, " ... the gift of God is eternal life (*zoe*) **through Jesus Christ our Lord**."

Romans 8:37, "Nay, in all these things we are more than conquerors **through Him** that loved us."

We are not just conquerors; we are MORE than conquerors.

I Corinthians 15:57, "But thanks be to God, which giveth us the victory **through our Lord Jesus Christ**."

Galatians 3:13-14, "Christ hath redeemed us from the curse of the law, being made a curse for us ... That the blessings of Abraham might come on the Gentiles **through Jesus Christ**; that we might receive the promise of the Spirit through faith."

Galatians 4:7, "Wherefore thou art no more a servant, but a son: and if a son, then an heir of God **through Christ**."

Ephesians 2:7, "That in the ages to come He might shew the exceeding riches of His grace in His kindness toward us **through Christ Jesus**."

Philippians 4:7, "And the peace of God, which passeth all understanding, shall keep your hearts and minds **through Christ Jesus**."

We do not have to worry, as God keeps our hearts and our minds.

Philippians 4:13, "**I can** do all things **through Christ** Who **strengthens** me." (In this passage, the Greek word for the phrase "I can" is *ischuō*, which is co-equally rendered *to exercise force, good, might, much work*. The word "strengthens" is the Greek word *endunamoō*, which is co-equally rendered *to empower.* The root word is *dunamis.*)

Look at Matthew 11:12, " ... the kingdom of heaven **suffereth** violence, **and the violent** take it by **force**." (In this passage, the Greek word for "suffereth" is *biazō*, which is co-equally rendered *to force.* In this passage, the phrase "and the violent" is the Greek word *bee-as-tace,* which is co-equally rendered *forcer, that is energetic.* The Greek word for "force" is *harpazo*, which is co-equally rendered *take by force.*)

Satan comes to steal, kill and destroy what God has given to us. We must "take by force" the blessings of the Kingdom of Heaven that are rightfully ours.

Hebrews 10:10, "By the which will **we are sanctified through** the offering of the body of **Jesus Christ** once for all." (In this passage, the Greek word for the phrase "we are sanctified" is *hagiazō*, which is co-equally rendered *to make holy, that is, purify or consecrate; be holy, sanctify.*)

I John 4:9, "In this was manifested the love of God toward us, because that God sent His only begotten Son into the world, that we might live **through Him**.

There is a divine lifestyle that can only be experienced by allowing Christ (which is God's Word) to live in you!

CHAPTER 5

BEING PERFECT

Jesus paid the price and God's Word is the document that validates that we can receive perfection when God's Word is applied to our lives.

"Nobody's perfect!" is a phrase that the church world has thrown around to excuse our mistakes and wrongdoings. The real foundational message of this phrase is, "Nobody's perfect, so, why try?" This suggests that you can do a lot of wrong things and still go to Heaven. Or, "Let's see how close to living like the devil you can live and still go to Heaven."

I'd rather we say, "How much like Jesus can we live and enjoy the very best of this life, and then go to Heaven and dance on streets of gold!"

We can live a perfect life, because Jesus paid the price for it. We may not arrive there overnight, but we can mature to it. We can do all things through Christ who strengthens us (Philippians 4:13)!

TELEIOS (*perfect*)

In the following passages, the Greek word for "perfect" is *teleios*, which is co-equally rendered *perfect man*. It is the same word used in reference to God being perfect.

Matthew 5:48, "Be ye therefore **perfect** (*teleios*) even as your Father which is Heaven is **perfect** (*teleios*)."

This is really a command from God. If God commands us to do something, then we *can* do it! However, an even greater truth from the heart of God is that this is an invitation to be perfect like God!

I Corinthians 2:6, "Howbeit we speak wisdom among them that are **perfect**."

The Apostle Paul was also speaking to us, today, as we live in the same dispensation.

I Corinthians 14:20, "**Brethren**, be not children in **understanding**: howbeit **in malice be ye children**, but in **understanding** be **men** (*teleios*)." (In this passage, the Greek word for "brethren" is *adelphos*, which is co-equally rendered *the womb*. The phrase "in malice" is *kakos*, which is co-equally rendered *trouble, injurious*. Both times the word "understanding" is used it is the Greek word *thphrēn*, which is co-equally rendered *of sympathy, the feelings (or sensitive nature; by extension [also in the plural] the mind or cognitive faculties*); the phrase "be ye children" is *nēpiazō*, which is co-equally rendered *to act as a babe, that is, innocently*.)

Translated using these Greek meanings, this passage would say, "Brothers and Sisters in the Lord, be not children of feelings or of a sensitive nature, howbeit, when you have trouble, be perfect."

Ephesians 4:13, "Till we all come in the unity of the faith, and of the knowledge of the Son of God, unto a **perfect** man, unto the measure of the stature of the fullness of Christ."

Verses 11-13 say that God has given gifts to the body of Christ (the church), apostles, prophets, evangelists, pastors and teachers for the perfecting of the body of Christ (today's Christians).

Philippians 3:15, "Let us therefore, as many as be **perfect**, be thus minded ..."

Colossians 1:28, "Whom we preach, warning every man, and teaching every man in all wisdom; that we may present every man **perfect** in Christ."

The purpose of the Apostle Paul's teaching and preaching was for the perfecting of Christians.

Colossians 4:12, "... that ye may stand **perfect** and complete in all of the will of God."

Since God is no respecter of persons (see Romans 2:11), this proclamation was made for New Testament people, which is everyone who has been born-again from the book of Acts through eternity.

Hebrews 5:14, "But strong meat belongeth **to them that are of full** age, even those who by reason of use have their senses exercised to discern both good and evil. (In this passage, the Greek word for the phrase "to them that are of full" is *teleios*.)

Verses 12-14 show why many people do not know right from wrong. This passage teaches us how we can know right from wrong, in addition to teaching us how to be perfect.

Hebrews 10:1, "For the law having a shadow of good things to come, and not the very image of the things, can never with those sacrifices which they offered year by year continually make the comers thereunto **perfect**."

Verse 14, "For by one offering He hath **perfected** for ever them that are sanctified."

There are many verses to validate that we are sanctified, if we have been born-again (see Hebrews 13:12).

Hebrews 7:19, "For the law made nothing **perfect** *(teleios)*, but the bringing in of a better hope did; by the which we draw nigh unto God."

As you read the book of Hebrews, you see that God is comparing the Old Testament with the New Testament. He is teaching us that the Old Testament could not make the make people **perfect**, but the New Testament does!

Hebrews 11:40, "God having provided some better thing for us, that they without us should not be made **perfect**."

Hebrews 13:20-21, "Now the God of peace...make you **perfect**."

James 1:4, "**But let patience** have her perfect work, that ye may be **perfect** and entire, wanting nothing." (In this passage, the Greek word for the phrase "But let patience" is *hupomonē*, which is co-equally rendered *endurance, constancy*.)

God's Word is declaring that perfection is ours, if we will receive it! We must initiate patience to be perfect.

James 3:2, "If any man **offend** not in word, the same is a **perfect** man and able also to bridle the whole body." (In this passage, the Greek word for "offend" is *ptaio*, which is co-equally rendered *to err, sin, fail, [of salvation] fall, offend, stumble,* and does not include the word "man" at all.)

KATARTIZO (*perfect*)

In the following passages, the word "perfect" comes from the Greek word "*katartizō*", which is used to describe us as perfect.

Luke 6:40, "The disciple is not above his master: but every one that is **perfect** shall be as his master."

Jesus is telling us that we should be like our Master (God).

II Corinthians 13:11, "Finally, brethren farewell. **Be perfect**, be of good comfort, be of one mind, live in peace, and the God of love and peace shall be with you."

Hebrews 13:21, "Make you **perfect** in every good work to do His will, working in you that which is well pleasing in His sight, through Jesus Christ; to Whom be glory for ever and ever, Amen."

I Peter 5:10, "But the God of all grace, Who hath called us unto His eternal glory by Christ Jesus, after that ye have suffered a while, make you **perfect**, stablish, strengthen, settle you."

II Timothy 3:16-17, "All Scripture is give so we can be profitable for righteousness. That the man of God may be **perfect**, thoroughly furnished." (In this passage, the Greek word for "perfect" is *artios,* which is co-equally rendered *perfect, complete.*)

CHAPTER 6

HAVING GOD'S REPUTATION

In the following passages, you will see how the use of the Greek word *doxa* validates us having God's glory and reputation, now. Keep in mind, the root word for "doxa" is *dokeo*, which is co-equally rendered be *accounted, be of reputation*.

John 17:22, "And the **glory** which Thou gavest me I have given them: that they may be one, even as We are one."

This was Jesus' prayer for us, today, and His prayers were always answered.

Romans 2:10-11, "But **glory,** honor and peace to every man that worketh good, to the Jew first, and also to the Gentile. For there is no respect of persons with God."

Romans 5:2, "By Whom also we have access by faith into this grace wherein we stand, and rejoice in hope of the **glory** of God."

By grace, we have access to stand in God's glory.

Romans 6:4, "Therefore we are buried with Him by baptism into death that like as Christ was raised up from the dead by the **glory** of the Father, even so we also should walk in newness of life (*zoe*)."

Jesus paid the price for us to walk in God's glory. This is this newness of life (*zoe*) that we *should* walk in.

Romans 8:18, "For I reckon that the **sufferings** of this time are not worthy to be compared with the **glory** which shall be revealed in us." (In this passage, the Greek word for "sufferings" is *pathema*, which is co-equally rendered *hardship*.)

There is a hardship on the flesh and mind to walk in holiness; but what a small price to pay for the privilege to walk in and live in the glory of God.

Romans 8:21, "Because the **Creature Itself** also shall be delivered from the bondage of corruption into the **glorious** liberty of the children of God." (In this passage, the Greek word for "creature" is *ktisis* with the root word of *ktizo*, which is co-equally rendered *Creator*. The Greek word for "itself" is *autos*, which is co-equally rendered *Himself*.)

The corruption of bondage that Jesus experienced was the cross, so we could freely have the glory of God.

Notice in verse 19, God has earnest expectation in waiting for the manifestations of the sons of God. For the sons of God to do what? For the sons of God to live in His **glory** while on the earth (see verses 11, 17-18, 21).

Romans 9:23-24, "And that He might make known the riches of His **glory** on the vessels of mercy, which He had afore prepared unto **glory**. Even us, whom He hath called!"

Romans 15:7, "Wherefore receive you one another as Christ also received us to the **glory** of God."

Christ already has received us into God's reputation, God's glory!

I Corinthians 2:7, "But we speak the wisdom of God in a mystery, even the hidden wisdom which God ordained before the world unto our **glory**!"

The mystery (the hidden wisdom that God ordained before the world began) is the glory of God that is to be experienced and lived on a daily bases by His children while living in this natural world. This mystery is a profound secret that can only be experienced when we are born-again and read and believe God's Word.

I Corinthians 2:9-10, "But as it is written, eye hath not seen, nor ear heard, neither have entered into the heart of man, the things which God hath prepared for them that love Him. But God hath revealed them unto us by His Spirit: for the Spirit searcheth all things, yea, the deep things of God."

You cannot separate the Spirit of God from the Word of God; they are the same thing. God's deep secrets are revealed from His Word (see John 1:1,14; 6:63)!

II Corinthians 1:20, "For all the promises of God in Him are yea, and in Him Amen, unto the **GLORY** OF GOD BY US!"

II Corinthians 3:7-11, "But if the ministration of death, written and engraven in stones, was **glorious**, so that the children of Israel could not steadfastly behold the face of Moses for the **glory** of his countenance; which **glory** was to be done away: How shall not the ministration of the spirit be rather **glorious**? For if the ministration of condemnation be **glory**, much more doth the ministration of righteousness exceed in **glory**. For even that which was made **glorious** had not **glory** in this respect, by reason of the **glory** that excelleth. For if that which is done away was **glorious**, much more that which remaineth is **glorious**."

II Corinthians 3:18, "But we all **with open face** beholding **as in a glass** the **glory** the of the Lord, are changed into the same image from **glory** to **glory**, even as by the Spirit of the Lord." (In this passage, the Greek word for the phrase "with open" is *anakaluptō*, which is co-equally rendered *uncovered*. The Greek word for "face" is *prosōpon*, which is co-equally rendered *person*. The phrase "as in a glass" is *katoptrizomai*, which is co-equally rendered *to mirror oneself, that is, to see reflected.*)

Verses 6-18 help us to better understand that the glory (reputation of God) that was seen on Moses is not to be compared with the GLORY that we have now! Jesus paid the price for this gift to be given to us; however, we must look into God's Word the same way we would look into a mirror and change ourselves. Looking in the mirror (God's Word), the influence of God's Word changes us to reflect God's reputation.

II Corinthians 4:1, "Therefore seeing we have this ministry ..."

The ministry that God gave us is His glory (His reputation). In the Greek and Hebrew, there are no chapters and verses, so II Corinthians 3:18 is the introduction of the ministry we have, which is God's glory.

II Corinthians 4:4, "In whom the god of this world hath blinded the minds of them which believe not, lest the light of the **glorious** Gospel of Christ, who is the image of God should shine unto them."

Satan has rights to blind the eyes of those that do not believe God's Word, keeping them from having God's glory.

II Corinthians 4:6, "For God, Who commanded the light to shine out of darkness, hath shined in our hearts, to give the light of the knowledge of the **glory** of God in the face of Jesus Christ."

Verse 11, "...that the life also of Jesus might be made manifest in our mortal flesh (our natural, earthly bodies)."

II Corinthians 4:15, "For all things are for your sakes, that the abundant grace might through the thanksgiving of many **redound** to the **glory** of God." (In this passage, the Greek word for "redound" is *perisseuō*, which is co-equally rendered *to super-abound or excel: exceed, abound, [have more] abundance.*)

II Corinthians 4:17, "For our light affliction, which is but for a moment, worketh for us a far more exceeding and eternal weight of **glory."**

The greater the trials or tests, the greater the opportunity to use and release God's glory!

Ephesians 1:6, "To the praise of the **glory** of His grace, wherein He hath made us accepted in the beloved."

God has accepted us into His glory.

Ephesians 1:18, "The eyes of your understanding being enlightened; that ye may know what is the hope of His calling, and what the riches of the **glory** of His inheritance in the saints."

The Apostle Paul was praying for the saints (the Christians at Ephesus), that they would have their understanding enlightened to know the riches of God's glory that belonged to them as Christians.

Today, we need to pray this prayer daily for ourselves and for others, as this is a deep mystery, a profound spiritual truth, impossible for any human mind to comprehend. By praying this prayer, we are changed from glory to glory by the Spirit of God (II Corinthians 3:18).

Ephesians 3:11-12 says that we are God's eternal purpose in Christ, and that Jesus paid the price for this reality.

Ephesians 5:27, "That He might present it to Himself a **glorious** church, not having spot, or wrinkle, or any such thing; but that it should be holy and without blemish."

God has provided the means for us to have the same perfection in our lives that He has in His own. The rapture will not take place until people experience this fact *in the flesh* (see my book entitled, Neglecting Signs and Wonders is Neglecting the Rapture.)

Philippians 3:21, "Who shall change our vile body, that it may be fashioned like unto His **glorious** body, according to the working whereby He is able even to subdue all things unto Himself."

Colossians 1:27, "To whom God would make known what is the riches of the **glory** of this mystery among the Gentiles: which is Christ in you, the hope of **glory**."

What an awesome passage of Scripture! There was a time when God had such hope in Jesus manifesting His reputation to humanity that He sent Him to this earth. God clearly knew that Jesus would have to pay the price in a most profound way, so that we (born-again Christians) could now be the hope of God being glorified in this world. This is the mystery, which was hid from the foundations of the world and is now manifested; this is now a reality. **We are the hope of God's reputation being exhibited in this world!**

I Thessalonians 2:12, "That ye would walk worthy of God, who **hath called** you unto His Kingdom and **glory**." (In this passage, the Greek word for the phrase "hath called" is *kaleō* with the root word being *keleu*, which is co-equally rendered *order, command*.)

We have been ordered and commanded by God to walk and live with His glory (*doxa*).

Again, by the highest authority in all of existence, we are ordered to obtain God's glory, His reputation!

II Thessalonians 2:14, "Whereunto he called you by our Gospel, to the obtaining of the **glory** (*doxa*) of our Lord Jesus Christ."

Again, another clear passage validating that God has "called" us to obtain His very reputation.

II Timothy 2:10, "Therefore I endure all **things for the elect's** sakes that they may also obtain the salvation which is in Christ Jesus with eternal **glory."** (In this passage, the Greek word for the phrase "things for the elect's" is *eklektos*, which is co-equally rendered *chosen*.)

Keep in mind, we are all chosen if we will accept (see I Peter 2:9). The Apostle Paul endured many things to make sure that Christians would obtain God's glory (God's reputation).

Hebrews 2:10, "For it became Him, for Whom are all things, and by Whom are all things, in bringing many **sons** unto **glory**, to make the captain of their salvation perfect through sufferings." (In this passage The Greek word for "sons" is *uihos*, which is co-equally rendered *children.*)

Jesus paid the price so that the children of God (Christians) could obtain God's glory.

I Peter 1:7, "That the trial of your faith, being much more precious than of gold that perisheth, though it be tried with fire, might be found unto praise and honour and **glory** at the appearing of Jesus Christ."

When the rapture takes place there will be a people that will be manifesting, living and experiencing God's glory!

I Peter 1:11, "Searching what, or what manner of time the Spirit of Christ which was in them did signify, when it testified beforehand the sufferings of Christ, and the **glory** that should follow."

Notice in verse 12, this Gospel (this Good News) is something that the angels know they cannot experience, but they desire just to look at it!

In verse 13, God is clearly telling us to study His Word, gird up the strength of your mind for this revelation of Jesus Christ.

Verses 15 & 16 give even more validity to verses 11-13, as God tells us we can have His reputation (His glory). He commands us and gives us the invitation to "BE HOLY, AS HE IS HOLY"!

I Peter 4:13, "But rejoice, inasmuch as ye are partakers of Christ's **suffering**, that, when His **glory shall be revealed** ye may be glad also with exceeding joy." (In this passage, the Greek word for "suffering" is *pathēma*, which is co-equally rendered *something undergone*. In this passage, the phrase "shall be revealed" is *apokalupsis,* which is co-equally rendered *manifestation*.)

When you pursue the reputation of God, there will be great persecution (see John 15:18-20). However, when the manifestation of God's glory is experienced in your life, the exceeding gladness and joy will ignore the persecution, as if it were nothing. The greater the persecution, the greater the glory!

I Peter 4:14, "If ye be reproached for the name of Christ, happy are ye; for the spirit of **glory** and of God resteth upon you: on their part he is evil spoken of, but on your part He is **glorified**."

I Peter 5:10, "But the God of all grace who hath called us unto His eternal **glory** by Christ Jesus after that ye have suffered a while, make you perfect, stablish, strengthen, settle you."

God calls us into His glory!

II Peter 1:3, "According as His divine power hath given unto us all things that pertain unto life and Godliness, through the knowledge of Him that hath called us to **glory** and virtue."

CHAPTER 7

WE ARE HOLY

Jesus' death paid the price for us to be holy. God desired to be in our presence and embrace us with His supernatural love, so He sent His only Son to die on the cross. Jesus' death paid the price for us to be holy, making it possible for us to be in God's presence.

These New Testament verses confirm that we are holy because of the price that Jesus paid.

HAGIOS (*holy*)

In the following verses, the Greek word for "holy" is *hagios*, which is co-equally rendered *sacred, physically pure, morally blameless or religious, ceremonially consecrated: [most] holy [one], saint.*

Acts 2:4, "And they were all filled with the **Holy** Ghost, and began to speak with other tongues, as the Spirit gave them utterance."

Jesus paid the price for us to be holy as God is holy. If we will receive the Holy Ghost and speak in tongues, holiness will be manifested in us. Holiness is ours; however, we must accept and receive it.

Acts 2:38, "Then Peter said unto them, Repent, and be baptized every one of you in the name of Jesus Christ for the remission of sins and ye shall receive the gift of the **Holy** Ghost."

Everyone can receive this holiness!

Acts 19:2, "He said unto them, have ye received the **Holy** Ghost since ye believed? And they said unto him, We have not so much as heard whether there be any **Holy** Ghost."

We are in the same dispensation. All we have to do is believe and receive the Holy Ghost.

Romans 3:28, "...we conclude that a man is **justified** by faith without the deeds of the law." (In this passage, the Greek word for "justified" is *dikaioō,* which is co-equally rendered *innocent.* The root word is *didaios,* which is co-equally rendered *holy [absolutely].*)

Romans 6:19, "...yield your members servants to righteousness unto **holiness**."

Romans 8:27, "And He that searcheth the heart knoweth what is the mind of the Spirit, because He maketh intercession for the **saints** according to the will of God."

In the mind of God, we are saints and we are holy! The word "saints" is written 61 times in the King James Version of the New Testament. The word *hagios* appears 157 times in the Greek text of the New Testament.

Romans 11:16, "For if the first fruit be **holy**, the lump is also **holy**: and if the root be **holy**, so are the branches."

I Corinthians 6:17, "...he or she that is joined unto the Lord is one spirit!"

Romans 12:1, "I beseech you therefore, brethren, by the mercies of God, that ye present your bodies a living sacrifice, **holy**, acceptable unto God, which is your reasonable service."

I Corinthians 3:17, "If any man defile the temple of God, him shall God destroy; for the temple of God is **holy**, which temple ye are."

The highest authority in all existence (God) says not only are we His temple, but we are holy!

I Corinthians 6:19, "What? know ye not that your body is the temple of the **Holy** Ghost which is in you, which ye have of God, and ye are not your own?"

II Corinthians 7:1, "Having therefore these promises ... let us ... perfect **holiness**..." (In this passage, the Greek word for "holiness" is *hagiosune*, which is co-equally rendered *physically pure, morally blameless or religious, [most] holy, saint.*)

II Corinthians 9:12, "For the **administration** of this service not only supplieth the want of the **saints** (*hagios*), but is abundant also by many thanksgivings unto God."

As you study this chapter, you will find the "administration" that this verse is talking about is giving offerings for the work of God. When we do this, it allows us to be in a position where our WANTS are supernaturally supplied. This can only occur, because we are holy!

Ephesians 1:4, "According as He hath chosen us in Him before the foundation of the world, that we should be **holy** and without blame before Him in love."

Before the foundations of the world, God's plan was to send Jesus to pay the price for us to be holy. It happened!

Ephesians 5:27, "That He might present it to Himself a glorious church, not having spot or wrinkle, or any such thing; but that it should be **holy** and without blemish."

(In my book entitled, Neglecting the Ministry of Signs & Wonders is Neglecting the Rapture, *I teach that there will be a people who will learn to live in God's holiness before the rapture takes place [see Ephesians 5:27].)*

Colossians 1:12, "Giving thanks unto the Father, which hath made us meet to be partakers of the inheritance of the saints in **light**." (In this passage, the Greek word for "light" is *phōs,* which is co-equally rendered *to shine or make manifest, especially by rays; fire or light.*)

God has already made us partakers of His holiness! It is God's gift to accept and receive. We have been made partakers of God's holiness and have the ability to manifest by rays of God's rays, fire and light (see Habakkuk 3:4, Amplified Bible version).

Colossians 1:22, "In the body of His flesh through death, to present you **holy** and unblameable and unreproveable in His sight."

Because Jesus sacrificed of His flesh on the cross, we are now HOLY! What an awesome God with depths of love that is beyond the human understanding. Do not try to figure it out, just receive it.

Colossians 1:26-27, "Even the mystery which hath been hid from ages and from generations, but now is made manifest to His saints. To whom God would make known what is the riches of the glory of this mystery among the Gentiles; which is Christ in you, the hope of glory."

Again, God is calling us (His saints) holy.

Colossians 3:12, "Put on therefore, as the elect of God, **holy** and beloved, bowels of mercies, kindness, humbleness of mind, meekness, longsuffering."

If someone gives a coat to keep me warm and protect me from the elements, I must put it on. God has given us the clothing of His holiness; we must put it on.

I Thessalonians 4:7, "For God hath not called us unto uncleanness, but unto **holiness**."

Hebrews 6:4, "For it is impossible for those who were once enlightened, and have tasted of the Heavenly gift, and were made partakers of the **Holy** Ghost."

Once we have been born-again by accepting Jesus Christ as our Lord and Savior, we are partakers of God's holiness!

Hebrews 9:8, "The **Holy** Ghost this signifying, that the way into the holiest of all was not yet made manifest, while as the first tabernacle was yet standing."

In the Old Testament there was no way for people to enter into a lifestyle of God's holiness. We can now, however, enter into this holy lifestyle, because of the price that Jesus paid.

Hebrews 12:10, "For they verily for a few days **chastened** us after their own pleasure; but He for our profit, that we might be partakers of His **holiness.**" (In this passage, the Greek word for "chastened" is *paideuō*, co-equally rendered *to train up a child, that is, educate, or (by implication) discipline, instruct, teach.*)

So, by His Word, God instructs and teaches us to be holy!

Hebrews 12:11, "Now no chastening for the present seemeth to be joyous, but grievous: nevertheless afterward it yieldeth the peaceable fruit of **righteousness** unto them which are exercised thereby." (In this passage, the Greek word for "righteousness" is *dikaiosune*, whose root word is *dikaios* or *holy*.)

Verse 9 plainly teaches us that our "Father of Spirits" corrects us spiritually, today. The greatest force of the spirit world is God's Word (see John 6:63). As we receive correction from God's Word, we then receive righteousness. This is something we must do. God is not going to do it; *we* must initiate it.

I Peter 1:15-16, "But as He which hath called you is **holy**, so be ye **holy** in all manner of conversation. Because it is written, Be ye **holy**; for I am **holy**."

God has commanded us to be holy. Even richer is that God is inviting us to be holy! Then, God tells us that His holiness can be perfected in our lives *by our conversation*. Psalm 19:14 is an excellent passage for perfecting holiness in our lives.

I Peter 2:5, "Ye also, as lively stones, are built up a spiritual house, a **holy** priesthood, to offer up spiritual sacrifices, acceptable to God by Jesus Christ."

I Peter 2:9, "But ye are a chosen generation, a royal priesthood, a **holy nation**, a peculiar people; that ye should show forth the praises of Him Who hath called you out of darkness into His marvelous **light**." (In this passage, the Greek word for "nation" is *ethnos*, which is co-equally rendered *a tribe; specifically (non-Jewish): Gentile, people*. The Greek word for "light" is *phōs*, meaning *to shine or make manifest, especially by rays; luminousness: fire, light.*)

Not only are we chosen by God to be holy as He is holy, but we are called of God to allow His miracle-working luminousness light to go from us into others for miracles!

Revelation 20:6, "Blessed and **holy** is he that hath part in the first resurrection: on such the second death hath no power, but they shall be priests of God and of Christ, and shall reign with Him a thousand years."

All of us who have accepted Jesus Christ as our Lord and Savior are "holy", and we will never experience the second death (the eternal death).

AMOMOS (*faultless*)

In the following Scripture passages, the words highlighted are derived from the Greek word *amomos,* which is rendered *faultless, without blame, unblameable, unblemished.*

Ephesians 1:4, "According as He hath chosen us in Him before the foundation of the world, that we should be holy and **without blame** before Him in love."

This is how God sees us, because of the brutal, savage torture that Jesus experienced on the cross for every human being. God sees us through blood-stained eyes!

Ephesians 5:27, "That He might present it to Himself a glorious church, not having spot, or wrinkle, or any such thing; but that it should be holy and **without blemish**."

The rapture will consist of a people who are living in the "Ephesians 5:27" condition, both spiritually and physically (see II Corinthians 3:18, 4:4, 5-7, 10-11, 15, 17-18).

Colossians 1:22, "In the body of His flesh through death, to present you holy and **unblameable** and **unreproveable** in His sight."

Jude 1:24, "Now unto Him that is able to keep you from falling, and to present you **faultless** before the presence of His glory with exceeding joy."

CHAPTER 8

WE ARE RIGHTEOUS

Because of the price that Jesus paid on the cross, we are now righteous. In the following Scripture passages, the highlighted words are derived from the Greek word *dokeo,* which is co-equally rendered *in character or act; by implication innocent, holy (absolutely or relatively) right.*

Jesus paid the price for us to be righteous and innocent of any ill will. He paid the price for everything about us to be *right.* Nothing is wrong with us at all, because Jesus paid that price.

Matthew 5:6, "Blessed are they which do hunger and thirst after **righteousness***:* for they shall be filled."

The decision is ours!

Matthew 6:33, "But **seek** ye first the Kingdom of God, and His **righteousness**; and all these things shall be added unto you." (In this passage, the Greek word for "seek" is *zeteodzay-teh'-o*, which co-equally means *desire, enquire, require.*)

God is a *good* God and has given us many things; however, God is also very wise and has set a law in operation that we must follow in order to receive righteousness.

It isn't any different than the law of receiving air. If you were suddenly under water, you would make getting air a requirement spiritually, mentally, and physically or you would die. You would do whatever it took to get air. Air is ours all of the time, but if we are in a position that we do not have any, we MUST make *getting air* a requirement in order to stay alive. If we want righteousness alive in our life, we MUST make *receiving righteousness* a requirement.

To spiritually require righteousness you must find Scripture to validate that righteousness is yours, and mentally accept it as you read it. There is nothing more spiritual than God's Word. Finally, you must physically *act* like it is true (this is no different than receiving the air that belongs to you).

Romans 1:17, "For therein is the **righteousness** of God revealed from faith to faith: as it is written; the just shall live by faith."

God's righteousness is already ours, and as we spend time with God through reading His Word and talking to Him, He reveals more of it to us.

Romans 3:22, "Even the **righteousness** of God which is by faith of Jesus Christ unto all and upon all them that believe: for there is no difference."

Romans 4:5, "But to him that worketh not, but believeth on Him that justifieth the ungodly, his faith is counted for **righteousness**."

Romans 4:6, "Even as David also describeth the blessedness of the man, unto whom God imputeth **righteousness** without by one man's offence death reigned by one; much more they which receive abundance of grace and of the gift of righteousness shall reign in life by One, Jesus Christ."

Adam's sin caused death and unrighteousness to reign in the world. How much more does the death of Jesus cause righteousness to reign, today?

Romans 5:21, "That as sin hath reigned unto death, even so might grace reign through **righteousness** unto eternal life by Jesus Christ our Lord."

Romans 6:13, "Neither yield ye your members as instruments of unrighteousness unto sin: but yield yourselves unto God, as those that are alive from the dead, and your members as instruments of **righteousness** unto God."

Who is more powerful God or the devil? Of course, God is more powerful. So, it is easier to yield to God's righteousness than it is to yield to satan's unrighteousness! The lie of the devil is that you have to do many religious acts in order to become even a little righteous. A thousand times, no! Righteousness is a gift that no human could ever attain by any means. It is based on *God's* goodness and not our own.

Romans 6:16, "Know ye not, that to whom ye yield yourselves servants to obey, his servants ye are to whom ye obey; whether of sin unto death, or of obedience unto **righteousness**?"

Romans 6:18-19, "Being then made free from sin, ye became the servants of **righteousness**. I speak after the manner of men because of the infirmity of your flesh: for as ye have yielded your members servants to uncleanness and to iniquity unto iniquity; even so now yield your members servants to **righteousness** unto holiness."

It is easier to yield to righteousness, than it is to yield to sin. If this were not true, then satan would be more powerful than God, and he is not!

Romans 9:30, "What shall we say then? That the Gentiles, which followed not after **righteousness,** have attained to **righteousness**, even the **righteousness** which is of faith."

Romans 10:4, "For Christ is the end of the law for **righteousness** to every one that believeth."

Because of Christ we are no longer under the law, but we are now of the dispensation of grace, and by grace we are righteous.

Romans 10:10, "For with the heart man believeth unto **righteousness**; and with the mouth confession is made unto salvation."

Romans 14:17, "For the Kingdom of God is not meat and drink; but **righteousness**, and peace, and joy in the Holy Ghost."

In Matthew 16:19, we find that Jesus gave us the keys to the kingdom of heaven, "**And I will give** unto thee the keys of the kingdom of heaven: and whatsoever thou shalt bind on earth shall be bound in heaven: and whatsoever thou shalt loose on earth shall be loosed in heaven." (In this passage, the Greek word for the phrase "and I will give" is *didōmi*. This word has no indication of the word "will" in it.)

Accurately translated, this verse would read, "And I give unto thee the keys of the kingdom of heaven..."

I Corinthians 1:30, "But of Him are ye in Christ Jesus, who of God **is made** unto us wisdom, and **righteousness**, and sanctification, and redemption." (In this passage, the Greek word for the phrase "is made" is *ginomai*, which is co-equally rendered *ordained to be*.)

We, by the grace of God, are ordained to be righteous.

I Corinthians 15:34, "Awake to **righteousness**, and sin not, for some have not the knowledge of God: I speak this to your shame."

II Corinthians 3:9, "For if the ministration of condemnation be glory, much more doth the ministration of **righteousness** exceed in glory."

The ministration of condemnation was for the people of the Old Testament, and the ministration of righteousness is for the people of the New Testament.

II Corinthians 5:21, "For He hath made Him to be sin for us, Who knew no sin; that we might be made the **righteousness** of God in Him."

II Corinthians 6:14, "Be ye not unequally yoked together with unbelievers: for what fellowship hath **righteousness** (Christians) with unrighteousness? and what communion hath light with darkness?"

II Corinthians 9:10, "Now he that ministereth seed to the sower both minister bread for your food, and multiply your seed sown, and increase the fruits of your **righteousness**."

God causes the righteousness that He has given us to increase. As we walk closer to the Lord, He reveals greater depths of His righteousness that He has already given us.

II Corinthians 9:10, "Now he that ministereth seed to the sower both minister bread for your food, and multiply your seed sown, and increase the fruits of your **righteousness**."

Galatians 2:21, "I do not frustrate the grace of God: for if **righteousness** come by the law, then Christ is dead in vain."

If we are not righteous, then Christ lived and died in vain.

Galatians 3:21-22, "Is the law then against the promises of God? God forbid: for if there had been a law given which could have given life, verily **righteousness** should have been by the law. But the Scripture hath concluded all under sin, that the promise by faith of Jesus Christ might be given to them that believe."

The Old Testament could not give us righteousness; however, Jesus paid the price for us to have a New

Covenant, which is the New Testament. This New Covenant gives us the grace to be righteous.

Ephesians 4:24, "And that ye put on the new man, which after God is created in **righteousness** and true holiness."

Ephesians 5:9, "For the fruit of the spirit is in all goodness and **righteousness** and truth."

Fruit grows. As we mature in the Lord, righteousness grows in our lives.

Ephesians 6:14, "Stand therefore, having your loins girt about with truth, and having on the breastplate of **righteousness**."

The Lord is telling us to put on righteousness, as we would a piece of armor that would cover our most vital organ, our heart. If the most vital part of our person is protected in time of battle, we may get wounded, but it will not be fatal!

Philippians 1:10-11, "That ye may approve things that are excellent ... being filled with fruits of **righteousness** ..."

II Timothy 3:16, "All Scripture is given by inspiration of God, and is profitable for doctrine, for reproof, for correction, for instruction in **righteousness**."

God's Scriptures are given to us that we may have instructions of how to allow His righteousness to consume our lives.

Hebrews 5:13, "For every one that useth milk is unskillful in the word of **righteousness**: for he is a babe."

A person must study the Scriptures to learn this mystery of the ages that belongs to us - **RIGHTEOUSNESS**.

Hebrews 12:11, "Now no **chastening** for the present seemeth to be joyous, but grievous: nevertheless, afterward it yeildeth the peaceable fruit of **righteousness** unto them which are exercised thereby." (In this passage, the Greek word for "chastening" is *paideia*, which is co-equally rendered *education or training; by implication disciplinary correction: instruction.*)

Sometimes God's instructions for a better life are hard on the flesh, especially if the flesh has been accustomed to things contrary to God's Word. Even though humans know that certain things are wrong for them and may destroy their health, their flesh has grown addicted to them and counts the loss of them as grief. But if we want to enjoy the best of this life and the life to come, we must be Spirit-ruled (Word of God-ruled) Christians.

I Peter 2:24, "Who His own self bore our sins in His own body on the tree, that we, being dead to sins, should live unto **righteousness**: by Whose stripes ye were healed."

God tells us that we should live righteous, because He has given us this gift.

I John 2:29, "If ye know that He is **righteous,** ye know that every one that doeth righteousness is born of Him."

If we are born-again (Romans 10:9-10), we are born as a righteous person.

DIKAIOS (*righteousness*)

In the New Testament, another Greek word for "righteousness" is *dikaios,* which is rendered *innocent, holy, right.*

The truth of *dikaios* being a reality in one's life, depends on the person knowing it, believing it, and accepting it. There is really no time element for the manifestation; it is simply up to the person's hunger to embrace *dikaios.*

I Corinthians 15:34, "**Awake** to **righteousness**, and sin not; for some have not the knowledge of God: I speak this to your shame." (In this passage, the Greek word for "awake" is *eknēphō*, which is co-equally rendered *to rouse oneself out of stupor*.)

Titus 2:12, "Teaching us that, denying ungodliness and worldly lusts, we should live soberly, **righteously**, and Godly, in this present world."

If a person living in poverty awoke one day to immeasurable riches, they would learn to live life in a new way. Thus, we who were poor in spirit must awaken to righteousness.

CHAPTER 9

OTHER SCRIPTURES

(*that say the same thing, but use different words*)

Although the Scripture is full of verses that establish the truth of how God has already given us all we need or desire in this life and the life to come, this chapter includes only the verses that show this truth in clarity.

Matthew 6:22, "The **light** of the **body** is the eye: if therefore thine **eye** be single, thy whole body shall be full of light." (In this passage, the Greek word for "light" is *phōteinos*, whose root word is *phos*, which is co-equally rendered *to shine or make manifest, especially by rays; fire, light.* The Greek word for "body" is *soma*, whose root word is *sozo*, which is co-equally rendered *safe, to save, that is, deliver or protect: heal, preserve, save (self), do well, be (make) whole.* The Greek word for "eye" is *opthalmos*, which is co-equally rendered *vision.* Its root word is *optomai*, co-equally rendered *to gaze, that is, with wide-open eyes, as at something remarkable;*

a watching from a distance: appear, look, see. Opomai is used many times in the Scriptures in reference to people having divine visions from the Lord.)

Using the fuller translations of this verse, we could translate it as, "If our natural eye (mental eye) and spiritual eye will become single (single-minded, see James 1:7-8), then our spirit, mind and body will be full of God's light (His Shekhinah Glory).

One of the best illustrations that the Lord has given me regarding single-minded praying and receiving God's glory is how a fire can ignite from the single focus of the sun through a magnifying glass. The sun is always there, but you can only use its power when you have an instrument (magnifying glass) and someone willing to focus on ONE thing.

We have the presence of Almighty God with us all of the time; however, He needs a person that is willing to be an instrument (like the magnifying glass) and someone who will focus. Then, you will have the power of the SON flowing through you.

God has already given us His Skekhinah Glory, and according to His Scriptures (His instructions), all we have to do to receive it is to yield to it.

Matthew 6:33, "But seek ye first the Kingdom of God, and His righteousness; and all these things shall be added unto you!"

Matthew 6:33 was the first verse I committed to memory. I was just 17 years old when I made a strong recommitment of my life to the Lord. I set out to memorize Scriptures, because I began to realize that God was smarter than any one in existence, and He gave me the privilege of having His Word (His directions for my life).

It took me a while to learn how to memorize Scripture, but I finally did it - and you can, too! The devil lies to us, saying that not just anyone can memorize Scripture; that it is a gift from God. However, through any given span of time, we memorize thousands, possibly millions of things concerning many different subjects (food, clothes, people, etc.). In fact, it is rather easy to memorize things that we like.

We must understand that God's Word supplies everything that we could possibly need or desire, and by memorizing His Word, we will have a strong key to seeking God and His Kingdom. Then, all these things (things that the ungodly will lie and steal to obtain) are simply added to us. We must not try to figure it out, just realize that God is smarter than we are, and He will take care of the adding. It may come in many different ways (money, ideas, favor, job promotion, business opportunities, etc.).

All things that pertain to this life and Godlikeness are already given to us. The key that unlocks the door to these things being materialized in one's life is falling in love with God (seeking His Kingdom and His righteousness).

All of these things are simply added to your life, because your heart is right. They are given to the whole world, but most people cannot see them, because their hearts are not right, which allows satan to blind their eyes (see II Corinthians 4:3-4).

In Matthew 9:6, Jesus told the paralyzed man to take up his bed. Notice that Jesus never touched or prayed for the man. The man simply acted like he had healing and arose. By activating God's power (when he acted like the Bible was true), he was instantly made whole. God did not pick him up. He had to make an effort to arise. This man took what was already his!

In Matthew 10:7-8, Jesus sent His twelve disciples out saying, "you go and preach ... you heal the sick, raise the dead, cast out devils."

I realize that this was a commission to His disciples; however, there are a host of Scriptures in the New

Testament, alone, that validate that every person has been given this same commission (see I John 4:17).

Matthew 11:12, "...the kingdom of **heaven** suffereth violence, and the violent take it by force."

As you study this passage, you will find that the "heaven" in reference here is satan's kingdom. Ephesians 6:12 gives us a glimpse of this truth when it teaches us that our warfare is with spiritual wickedness in **high** places. (In this passage, the Greek word for "high" is *epouranios*, which is co-equally rendered *heavenlies.*)

Matthew 16:19, "And I will give unto thee the keys of the kingdom of heaven: and whatsoever thou shalt bind on earth shall be bound in heaven: and whatsoever thou shalt loose on earth shall be loosed in heaven."

God has given us the power and authority to bind satan's kingdom, in regards to stopping things that are contrary to God's promises. We, also, have the authority to loose blessings that are not yet a reality to us in this natural world, but are documented by God in His Word.

If we have this kind of authority, then we most definitely have already been given everything that pertains to life and Godliness in this world. We simply need to receive and exercise our rights.

Matthew 18:18 gives the same teaching as Matthew 16:19, "Whatsoever ye shall bind on earth shall be bound in heaven..."

If we bind things that are bad on earth, these same things will be bound in the realm of the heavenlies (satan's kingdom) (see Ephesians 6:12).

Matthew 21:21, "Jesus answered and said unto them, Verily I say unto you, If ye have faith, and doubt not, ye shall not only do this which is done to the fig tree, but also if ye shall say unto this mountain, Be thou removed, and be thou cast into the sea; it shall be done."

In order for this verse to be true (and it is!), we would have to have the power of God.

Matthew 25:21, 23, "... thou hast been faithful over a few things, I will make thee ruler over many things: enter thou into the joy of thy Lord."

The same joy that God experiences belongs to us, right now. All we have to do to receive it is to be faithful.

Mark 3:5, "Jesus told the man to stretch forth his hand."

By his actions, the man received what was already his.

Mark 4:13, "Know the parable and understand and know all of the **parables**." (In this passage, the Greek word for "parable" is *parabole,* which is co-equally rendered *proverb*. The dictionary says a proverb is a *practical truth*.)

There isn't a more practical truth than God's Word. In understanding the parable that Jesus taught in Mark 4, you see that when God's Word has been sown, satan comes immediately to steal it! Understanding this practical truth allows you to know all of truths of God, which already belong to us!

Mark 4:20, "And these are they which are sown on good ground; such as *hear the word, and receive it, and bring forth fruit,* some thirty-fold, some sixty, and some an hundred."

In order to receive into our natural reality the blessings that have already been given us, we must hear, accept and act like God's Word is true.

In Mark 5:27, the woman with the issue of blood TOUCHED Jesus and was instantly made whole. She activated God's power (that was already hers) by acting like God's Word was true!

Mark 9:23 says, "...all things are possible to him that believeth."

Mark 10:27, "...for with God all things are possible."

Just be "with God" (which is also His Word, John 1:1), and all things are possible for you.

Mark 10:29, "And Jesus answered and said, Verily I say unto you, There is no man that hath left house, or brethren, or sisters, or father, or mother, or wife, or children, or lands, for my sake, and the gospel's, but he shall receive a hundredfold now in this time, houses, and brethren, and sisters, and mothers, and children, and lands, with persecutions; and in the world to come eternal life."

Giving activates God's "hundredfold" blessing.

Mark 11:23, "Whosoever shall say unto this mountain, be thou removed..."

Mark 12:24, "...ye **know** not the Scriptures, neither the power of God?" (In this passage, the Greek word for "know" is *eido*, which is co-equally rendered *be aware, look on, understand.*)

By knowing God's Word, we can be aware of His power.

Mark 16:17, "...these **signs** shall follow them that believe..." (In this passage, the Greek word for "signs" is *semeion*, which is co-equally rendered *supernatural* *miracles in the senses realm confirming the atoning work of Christ.*)

Luke 1:37, "For with God, nothing shall be impossible."

We are with God at all times, as He said he would never leave us nor forsake us. Therefore, nothing is impossible for us (see Hebrews 13:5).

Luke 6:38, "(YOU) give and it shall be given unto you ... shall men give into your bosom..."

The blessing of receiving is giving.

Luke 6:47-48, "Whosoever cometh to Me, and heareth My sayings, and doeth them, I will show you to whom he is like: He is like a man which built a **house**, and digged deep, and laid the foundation on a rock: and when the flood arose, the stream beat vehemently upon that house, and could not shake it: for it was founded upon a rock." (In this passage, the Greek word for "house" is *oikia*, which is co-equally rendered *family.*)

Coming to Jesus, and HEARING and DOING His words will put you in a position where nothing can harm your house.

Luke 8:10-11, "...unto YOU IT IS GIVEN to know the mysteries of the Kingdom of God ... Now the parable is this: The seed is the Word of God" (see verses 12-15).

Luke 8:48, "...Daughter, thy faith hath made thee whole."

Faith is trusting and acting on God's Word, which activated this woman's miracle. God had already given her healing, so when she acted on God's Word, her body was healed!

Luke 9:62, "...No person, having put their hand to the plough, and looking back, is **fit** for the Kingdom of God." (In this passage, the Greek word for "fit" is *euthetos*, which is co-equally rendered *well-placed, conceive, set.*)

In this passage, Jesus is teaching that if a person is not single-minded, they cannot fit into God's Kingdom.

Imagine, if you will, the most awe-inspiring picture of beauty. Now, put yourself in the middle of that picture, owning everything a person could possibly need our desire. Now, take yourself out of the picture, as if this were a completed puzzle, and try to put your piece back in upside down and backwards. It simply does not fit.

When we are double-minded, we will never fit into the wonderful picture of all of God's blessings that belong to us. God has done His part; our part is simply fitting into what God has given us.

Luke 10:9, "...you heal the sick."

We have to have God's power to be able to heal the sick!

Luke 10:19, "Behold, I give unto you **power** to tread on serpents and scorpions, and over all the **power** of the enemy: and nothing shall by any means hurt you." (In this passage, the Greek word for "power" is *exousia*, which is co-equally rendered *delegated authority*.)

By our own abilities and strengths, we do not have power over the devil. An example of this is when a police officer stands in front of a huge tractor-trailer truck and simply lifts up their hand to demand the truck to stop. As a result, the truck will stop. Not because of the police officer's physical power, but because of the "delegated authority" of the country in which they are a representative.

In like manner, when we use the name of Jesus, we are clothed in the Spirit with the clothing of God. If satan or his adverse circumstances try to overrun us, they know they will have to face the highest court in all of existence, the Almighty Creator God! You have been given this delegated authority; however, if you do not know that you have it or how to activate it, it is useless for you.

Jesus taught us how to pray in Luke 11:2, "When ye pray, say, Our Father which art in Heaven, Hallowed be

Thy name. Thy Kingdom come. Thy will be done, as in Heaven, so in earth."

God gives us the privilege of establishing things on earth as they are in Heaven. We simply need to exercise our God-given rights.

Luke 11:34, "The light of the body is the eye: therefore when thine eye is single, thy whole body also is full of light; but when thine eye is evil, thy body also is full of darkness" (see Matthew 6:22).

Luke 17:6, "And the Lord said, If ye had faith as a grain of mustard seed, ye might say unto this sycamore tree, Be thou plucked up by the root, and be thou planted in the sea; and it should obey you."

The power has already been given to us. If we want to utilize it, we must exercise our faith, trust, believe, and have confidence in God's Word. Another example is the power of electricity in our homes. If we do not walk over and turn on the switch, it will be useless to us.

Luke 17:14, "And when He saw them, He said unto them, Go show yourselves unto the priests. And it came to pass, that, *as they went,* they were cleansed."

The ten lepers received what was already theirs by acting like Jesus' words were true.

Luke 17:21, "Neither shall they say, Lo here! or, lo there! For, behold, the Kingdom of God **is within** you." (In this passage, the Greek word for the phrase "is within" is *entos*, which is co-equally rendered *almost, about, shortly*.)

Jesus was teaching the Pharisees that the Kingdom of God would be in all people after they receive the new birth. So, if Jesus Christ is the Lord of our life, we have everything we could possibly need or desire inside of our spirits. If we want these things to come into the natural world, we must obey some spiritual and natural laws of God.

John 1:12, "... as many as received Him, to them gave He power to become the sons of God, even to them that believe on His name."

John 1:16, "And of His fullness have all **we received**..." (In this passage, the Greek word for the phrase "we received" is *lambano*, which is co-equally rendered *to have offered*.)

John 6:28-29, "What shall we do, that we might work the works of God? Jesus answered and said unto them, This is the work of God, that ye believe on Him Whom He hath sent."

What a simple solution to all of humanities' problems!

John 7:37-39, "He that believeth on Me, as the Scripture hath said, out of his belly shall flow rivers of living water. But this spake He of the Spirit, which they that believe on him should receive: for the Holy Ghost was not yet given; because that Jesus was not yet glorified."

Receiving the Holy Spirit with the evidence of speaking in tongues is receiving rivers of living waters that come from the Spirit of God (see Acts 2:4).

John 8:31-32, "If ye continue in My word, then are ye My disciples indeed; And ye shall know the truth, and the truth shall make you free."

Continuing in God's Word causes an activation of what belongs to the whole human race.

John 8:47, "He that is of God heareth God's words: ye therefore hear them not, because ye are not of God."

When you are a child of God, you hear God's voice, His Words. Keep in mind that God's Words are His power (Romans 1:16). So, hearing God's voice *is* receiving God's power.

John 8:51, "Verily, verily, I say unto you, If a man keep My saying, he shall never see death."

The person that keeps God's Words activates a supernatural life style that will never end.

John 10:28, "...My sheep hear My voice and they follow Me."

We have already been given the privilege to hear God's voice.

John 10:27, "My sheep hear My voice, and I know them, and they follow Me."

John 11:26, "And whosoever liveth and believeth in Me shall never die..."

John 14:12, "Verily, verily, I say unto you, He that believeth on Me, the works that I do shall he do also; and greater works than these shall he do; because I go unto My Father."

Believing activates the power of God that has been given to us. The ONLY way we could ever do the works of Jesus (and greater) is if everything that was given to Jesus is given to us.

John 14:27, "Peace I leave with you, My peace I give unto you: not as the world giveth, give I unto you. Let not your heart be troubled, neither let it be afraid."

God has already given us a peace that passes all understanding, and if we will accept it, fear and trouble will never overtake us.

John 15:3, "Now ye are **clean** through the word which I have spoken unto you. (In this passage, the

Greek word for "clean" is *katharos,* which is co-equally rendered *pure.*)

John 15:5, "...He that abideth in Me, and I in him, the same bringeth forth much fruit: for without Me ye can do nothing."

With Christ in us, we can bring forth the fruit of all of God's promises. Keep in mind, God's Word is co-equally Christ (see John 1:1-14). It is up to us to allow God's Word to be active in us.

John 15:8, "Herein is My Father glorified, that ye bear much fruit..."

It is the Father's perfect will that we bear fruit.

John 15:10-11, "...keep My commandments ... that My joy might remain in you."

God has already given us His commandments (His Word). As we keep and apply them in our lives, His love rules in us, and His joy remains in us.

John 17:18, "...as Jesus was sent, now are we sent."

Everything that was given to Jesus has been given to us.

John 20:23, "Whosoever sins ye remit they are remitted and whosever sins ye retain they are retained."

We have been given the privilege to forgive people's sins, with the exception of the sin of rejecting Jesus as Lord and blasphemy of the Holy Spirit (see I John 5:14-16; I Peter 2:9).

Acts 1:8, "...ye shall receive power, after the Holy Ghost is come upon you: and ye shall be witnesses."

The Holy Spirit has already been given to us , so all we have to do is *go* with the miracle-working power of God (see John 7:37-39, 14:16, 17:26; Acts 2:4, 38-39).

Acts 2:4, "THEY SPAKE in tongues as the Spirit gave them utterance."

They initiated the power of God, when they spoke. We have the same covenant rights, today.

Acts 2:25, "David speaketh concerning **Him, I foresaw** the Lord always before my face, for He is on my right hand that I should not be moved." (In this passage, the Greek word for the phrase "him, I foresaw" is *prooroo,* which means *to see, to mentally have a vision.*)

If you study visions from a Scriptural standpoint, you will find that *this* sort of a vision is the highest order of visions. It is the same type of vision as in Proverbs 29:18 (the type that is personally initiated).

In the Bible, David personally initiated seeing the Lord before him at all times, and this gave him supernatural victory at all times. We can and should do the same thing. God has given us the wonderful privilege of initiating it any time that we desire!

Acts 3:6, "...silver and gold have I none but in the name of Jesus rise and be healed."

Peter released the miracle-working power of God that was in him (that is in us).

Acts 3:16, "And His name through faith in His name hath made this man strong, whom ye see and know: yea, the faith which is by Him hath given him this perfect soundness in the presence of you all."

This man was made whole, because he acted like the Bible was true. True faith is a combination of believing the Bible and natural actions (see James 2:19-22).

Acts 5:12, 15-16, "...by the hands of the apostles were many signs and wonders wrought among the people ... Insomuch that they brought forth the sick into the streets, and laid them on beds and couches, that at the least the shadow of Peter passing by might overshadow some of them ... There came also a multitude out of the cities round about unto Jerusalem, bringing sick folks, and them which were vexed with unclean spirits: and they were healed EVERY ONE."

These verses show that the Apostles had the power of God in their lives. We are of the same dispensation as the Apostles, and Acts 10:34 says that Jesus Christ is the same yesterday, today and forever. There is no "respecter of persons" with God, so we also have this same ability.

Acts 8:6, "...the people gave heed unto those things which Philip spake, hearing and seeing the miracles which he did."

We have the same promises as Philip!

Mark 16:17, "... these **signs** shall follow those that believe." (In this passage, the Greek word for "signs" is *semeion*, which is co-equally rendered as *supernatural miracles in the senses realm confirming the atoning work of Christ.*)

Acts 8:13, "Then Simon himself believed also: and when he was baptized, he continued with Philip, and **wondered**, beholding the miracles and signs which were done ... Simon wondered because of seeing the miracles and signs which were done." (In this passage, the Greek word for "wondered" is *existemi*, which means *became astounded, amazed.*)

In Acts 8:9, we see that Simon had previously been used by demonic spirits for sorcery and witchcraft, but when he experienced the supernatural miracles and signs of the Almighty God displayed through Philip, he became a Christian, was baptized, and followed Philip's ministry.

Today, as never before, Christians need to live this type of lifestyle, which no false religion or carnal church program can re-produce. We need to have the power of God displayed in our lives, so that it breaks the demonic stronghold off of people's lives. **We must be CHRIST-LIKE, to the point that people are astounded and amazed at the power of God.** This type of ministry (that belongs to us all) will bring people to true salvation. When people truly get saved, they are also truly delivered from sin and all of its bondages (as "deliverance" and "salvation" are exactly the same word in the Greek and Hebrew).

Acts 9:33, "...Aeneas which had kept his bed eight years and was sick of the **palsy**." (In this passage, the Greek word for "palsy" is *paraluo*, which is co-equally rendered *paralyzed*.)

Acts 9:34-35, "...Peter said unto him, Aeneas, Jesus Christ maketh thee whole: arise, and make thy bed. And he arose immediately ... and ALL that dwell at Lydda and Saron saw him and turned to the Lord."

Mark 16:17 belongs to you as much as it belonged to Peter.

Acts 9:36-41, "Tabitha ... died ... Peter said, Tabitha arise ... he lifted her up!"

You have to act like God's Word is true, if you want to see It come to manifestation.

Paul and Barnabas went to Iconium, and in Acts 14:3, "... signs and wonders were done by their hands."

Acts 14:8, "a certain man cripple from his mother's womb, who never had walked ... (v. 10) ... Paul said with a loud voice, Stand upright on thy feet. And he leaped and walked."

Actions activate God's power.

In Acts 14:19, certain Jews from Antioch and Iconium persuaded the people to stone Paul, leaving him for dead. But in verse 20, Paul rose up; God has given us authority over death (see Matthew 10:8; I John 4:4).

Acts 15:12, "... the multitude kept silence, and gave audience to Barnabas and Paul, declaring what miracles and wonders God had wrought among the Gentiles by them."

We also have this same power, where multitudes will be drawn to Jesus Christ.

Acts 16:18, "But Paul, being grieved, turned and said to the spirit, I command thee in the name of Jesus Christ to come out of her. And he came out that same hour."

Acts 19:6, "And when Paul had laid his hands upon them, the Holy Ghost came on them; and they spake with tongues and prophesied."

We have the same power as in Acts 19:12, "So that from his body were brought unto the sick handkerchiefs or aprons, and the diseases departed from them, and the evil spirits went out of them."

In Acts 20:9-12, when Paul was long preaching, a young man fell into a deep sleep and fell down from third loft window, and was taken up dead. Paul embraced him, and the young man rose from the dead.

The Bible is our example. What God did through others is the example we are to follow.

Acts 26:8, "Why should it be thought a thing incredible with you, that God should raise the dead?"

Acts 27:10, "And said unto them, Sirs, I perceive that this voyage will be with hurt and much damage, not only of the landing and ship, but also of our lives."

Paul did not say, "the Lord told me," instead he said, "I PERCEIVE." The voice of God is speaking to our spirits at all times.

In Acts 28:3-6, Paul had gathered a bundle of sticks and a venomous beast (poisonous snake) hung on his hand. He should have died, but no harm came to him.

Mark 16:18 was true for Paul, and it is true for us today, "They shall take up serpents; and if they drink any deadly thing, it shall not hurt them; they shall lay hands on the sick, and they shall recover."

We do not have a dead Gospel. It is alive for now and forevermore!

Romans 2:29, "But he is a Jew, which is one inwardly; and circumcision is that of the heart, in the spirit, and not in the letter..."

Romans 3:1-2, "What ADVANTAGE then hath the Jew? ... unto them were committed **the oracles** of God." (In this passage, the Greek word for the phrase "the oracles" is *logion*, which is co-equally rendered *the words or utterances of God.*)

We are of the same dispensation, and have the same advantage. We are God's chosen, because we follow the whole counsel of God.

Romans 3:4, "...That thou mightiest be justified in thy sayings, and mightiest overcome when thou art judged."

We have this privilege, because we are the very children of God!

Romans 3:22, "...the righteousness of God which is by faith of Jesus Christ unto ALL and upon ALL them that believe."

Romans 3:28, "...we conclude that a man is **justified** by faith without the deeds of the law." (In this passage, the Greek word for "justified" is *dikaioo*, which is co-equally rendered *innocent, holy, righteous.*)

Just as an American Indian belongs to a tribe (not because he has purchased or earned his heritage, but because he was simply born into it), when we accept Jesus Christ as our Lord, we are simply born into the divine family of God. We are children of God!

Romans 4:5, "But to him that worketh not, but believeth on him that justifieth the ungodly, his faith is counted for righteousness."

Romans 4:6, "...the blessedness of the man, unto whom God imputeth righteousness without works."

This is a divine blessing, which is impossible to earn, as it is a gift from God (see Ephesians 2:8-9).

Romans 4:24-25, "But for us also, to whom it shall be imputed, if we believe on Him that raise up Jesus our

Lord from the dead; Who was delivered for our offences, and was raised again for our justification."

Romans 5:1, "Therefore being justified by faith, we have peace with God through our Lord Jesus Christ."

Romans 5:11, "...through our Lord Jesus Christ, by Whom we have now received the atonement."

Romans 5:15, "...through the offence of one many be dead, much more the grace of God, and the gift by grace, which is by One man, Jesus Christ, hath abounded unto many."

Romans 5:16, "...the free gift is of many offences unto justification."

Romans 5:17, "For if by one man's offence death **reigned** by one; much more they which receive abundance of grace and of the gift of righteousness shall **reign** in life by One, Jesus Christ." (In this passage, the Greek word for "reign" is *basileuo*, which is co-equally rendered *to reign as a king*.)

Romans 6:5, "For if we have been planted together in the likeness of His death, we shall be also in the likeness of His resurrection."

Romans 6:13, "...**yield** yourselves unto God, as those that are alive from the dead, and your members as instruments of righteousness unto God." (In this passage, the Greek word for "yield" is *paristemi*, co-equally rendered as *stand beside, command, present, prove, provide.* The dictionary defines this as *surrender.*)

We need to command our lives to be instruments of righteousness (see I Corinthians 5:21).

Romans 6:19, "...yield your members servants to righteousness unto holiness."

Romans 8:3, "For what the law could not do, in that it was weak through the flesh, God sending His own Son in the likeness of sinful flesh, and for sin, condemned sin in the flesh: That the righteousness (*dikaios*) of the law might be fulfilled in us, who walk not after the flesh, but after the Spirit."

Romans 8:11, "But if the Spirit of Him that raised up Jesus from the dead dwell in you, He that raised up Christ from the dead shall also **quicken** your mortal bodies by His Spirit that dwelleth in you." (In this passage, the Greek word for "quicken" is *zoopoieo*, which is co-equally rendered *to restore to life, endued with new and greater powers of life.*)

Romans 8:16, "The Spirit Himself beareth witness with our spirit, that we are the children of God."

Romans 8:17, "And if children, then heirs; heirs of God, and joint-heirs with Christ; if so be that we suffer with Him, that we may be also **glorified** together." (In this passage, the Greek word for "glorified" is *doxazo*, whose root word is *dokeo*, which is co-equally rendered *be of reputation*.)

Because of Christ, we have the reputation of God!

Romans 8:19, "For the earnest expectation of the **Creature** waiteth for the manifestation of the sons of God. (In this passage, the Greek for "creature" is *ktisis*, whose root word is *ktizo*, which is co-equally rendered *Creator*.)

For over 2,000 years, people have been waiting for God to produce manifestations. And for 2,000 years, God is still waiting on us to use what He has already given us!

Romans 8:32, "He that spared not His own Son, but delivered Him up for us all, how shall He not with Him also freely **GIVE US ALL THINGS!"**

Romans 9:30, "...the Gentiles, which followed not after righteousness, have attained to righteousness, even the righteousness which is of faith."

God has given righteousness to the entire human race. What a shame for people to live like paupers, spiritually, mentally, socially and financially, when the price has been paid for them to live like kings and queens (see Revelation 19:16). Worse, yet, is that many have needlessly gone to hell. You shall know the truth, and the truth shall set you free!

Romans 10:4, "...righteousness to everyone that believeth."

Romans 10:10, "...with heart believeth unto righteousness."

Romans 12:2, "...be ye **transformed**." (In this passage, the Greek word for "transformed" is the exact Greek word for "transfigured" also found in Mark 9:2.)

Romans 13:14, "*...put ye on* the Lord Jesus Christ."

Romans 15:29, "...I shall come in the fullness of the blessing of the Gospel of Christ."

Romans 16:25-26, "Now to Him that is of power to stablish you according to my Gospel, and the preaching of Jesus Christ, according to the revelation of the mystery, which was kept secret since the world began, But now is made manifest, and by the Scriptures of the prophets, according to the commandment of the everlasting God, made known to all nations for the obedience of faith" (see Colossians 1:26-27).

I Corinthians 1:5, "...we are enriched by Him in everything!"

I Corinthians 1:7, "ye come behind in no gift."

I Corinthians 2:4, "And my speech and my preaching was not with enticing words of man's wisdom, but in demonstration of the Spirit and of power."

By the authority of the abundance of Scripture in this book, we all can do this same thing! The Apostle Paul came not with just a great sermon, but with demonstration of the miracle-working power of God, so that people's faith would stand in the power of God, not the intellect of a human. Keep in mind, everything that was given to Apostle Paul has been given to us.

I Corinthians 2:9-10 says that God has revealed the deep things of Himself to us!

I Corinthians 2:12, "Now, we have received not the spirit of the world, but the Spirit which is of God; that we might know things that are freely given to us of God."

I Corinthians 3:9, "...we are labourers together with God."

I Corinthians 3:16, "Know ye not that ye are temple of God, and that the Spirit of God dwelleth in you?"

I Corinthians 4:8, "...ye are rich and reign as kings."

I Corinthians 6:17, "But he that is joined unto the Lord is one spirit."

I Corinthians 6:19, "...your body is the temple of the Holy Ghost."

I Corinthians 7:14, "...now are you holy."

I Corinthians 12:7, "...manifestation of the Spirit is given to every man."

THE GIFTS OF THE HOLY SPIRIT ARE FOR EVERYONE

I CORINTHIANS

I Corinthians 12:7-11, "But the manifestation of the Spirit is **given to every man** to profit withal. For to one is given by the Spirit the word of wisdom; **to another** (*allos* – in the Greek co-equally rendered as *that is, one another*) the word of knowledge by the same Spirit; **To another** (*heteros* – in the Greek co-equally rendered as *next quality, one another*) faith by the same Spirit; **to another** (*allos*) the gifts of healing by the same Spirit; **To another** (*heteros*) the working of miracles; **to another** (*allos*) prophecy; **to another** (*allos*) discerning of spirits; **to another** (*heteros*) divers kinds of tongues; **to another** (*allos*) the interpretation of tongues: But all these worketh that one and the selfsame Spirit, dividing to every man severally **as he will** (*boulomai* – in the

Greek co-equally rendered *be willing, be minded, choose, desire.*)"

Looking closer at the phrase "as he will", the word "he" in this passage is an antecedent pronoun which always refers to the closest noun that proceeds it. In this case, it would be the word *man.*

Notice the introduction of this teaching starts in verse 7, "...the manifestation of the Spirit is **given to every man** to profit withal."

Looking at the Greek renderings in this passage (along with the context of the Scriptures) we could read, "But the manifestation of the Spirit is given to every man to profit withal. **In fact/indeed** is given by the Spirit the word of wisdom**; that is** the word of knowledge by the same Spirit; **Next,** faith by the same Spirit; **that is for one another** the gifts of healing by the same Spirit; **That is, for one another** the working of miracles; **that is for one another** prophecy; **that is for one another** discerning of spirits; **next for quality,** divers kinds of tongues; **that is for one another** the interpretation of tongues: But all these worketh that one and the selfsame Spirit, dividing to every man severally **that is willing, that chooses, that desires**."

I Corinthians 12:31, "...covet earnestly the best gifts."

Why would God tell us to covet the "gifts", if they would only be given to certain people? God wants us to desire all of the gifts of the Holy Spirit (see I Corinthians 14:1)!

I Corinthians 14:5, "I would that ye all spake with tongues but rather that ye prophesied."

God's perfect will is His Word. According to His perfect will, He desires for all of us to speak in tongues and prophesy.

I Corinthians 14:15, "I will pray with the spirit ... I will sing with the spirit."

Once we have been filled with the Holy Spirit with the evidence of speaking in tongues (as Acts 2:4 records), we can speak in tongues at will. Speaking in tongues is a supernatural gift whose purpose is for us to be supernaturally edified and speak divine secrets to God (see I Corinthians 14:2).

I Corinthians 14:39, "...covet to prophecy..."

God is telling us that we can all prophecy, as He is telling us all to desire to prophecy.

I Corinthians 15:16-17, "For if the dead rise not, then is not Christ raised: and if Christ be not raised, your faith is vain."

God is telling us that if we cannot raise the dead, our faith is vain/empty. If our faith is vain, then we do not have salvation and without salvation cannot enter the Kingdom of Heaven.

Raising people from the dead is one of the BASIC doctrines of Christ (see Hebrews 6:1-2). Also, notice in Matthew 10:6-8, when Jesus sent His disciples out, He gave them BASIC instructions, one of which was raising the dead.

John 17 tells us that Jesus prayed for us that believe (verse 20). He prayed that as God sent Him, so does He now send us into the world (verse 18). He prayed that the same **glory** (*doxa*) that God gave Him would be given to us! Jesus always got His prayers answered, so, we NOW HAVE THE VERY REPUTATION OF JESUS (and Jesus raised the dead).

I Corinthians 15:34, "Awake to righteousness, and sin not; for some have not the knowledge of God: I speak this to your shame."

To have the knowledge of God is to simply read His Word. If we read It, we will find that we are the righteousness of God (II Corinthians 5:21, "For He hath made Him to be sin for us, Who knew no sin; that we might be made the righteousness of God in Him!").

II CORINTHIANS

In II Corinthians 3:7-18 God tells us that the very reputation of God that Moses experienced had NO GLORY compared to the **glory** (*doxa*) that has been given to us, because of the price that Jesus paid on the cross. It will be a natural and spiritual reality to all who will look in the mirror of God's Word and arrange themselves accordingly!

II Corinthians 4:1, "Therefore seeing we have this ministry, as we have received."

What ministry do we have? We have the ministry that the previous verses (3:7-18) just finished telling us about - the ministry of having the very reputation of Jesus!

II Corinthians 4:6-7, "For God, Who commanded the light to shine out of darkness, hath shined in our hearts, to give the light of knowledge of the **glory** (*doxa*) of God in the face of Jesus Christ. But we have **this treasure** in earthen vessels, that the excellency of the power may be of God, and not of us."

"This treasure" is the reputation of God, as all the verses leading up to this verse have clearly taught us. The earthen vessels are our natural bodies, our mortal flesh (see verses 7, 10-11).

A secret that everyone must know is that God's Word is truth, not because you see it or feel it, but because God said it. When it is more real to you in the spiritual than the natural, it will show up in the natural. Many times we exalt and worship the natural more than the spiritual, which is why we do not have it in the natural. II Corinthians 10:4-5 tells us that our warfare is not of this natural world, it is of the spirit world. To fight against this demonic spirit world, one must first cast down these demonic strongholds (knowledge that is against the knowledge of God's Word).

II Corinthians 4:15, "For all things are for your sakes, that the abundant grace might through the thanksgiving of many **redound** to the **glory** (*doxa*) of God." (In this passage, the Greek word for "redound" is *perisseuo*, which is co-equally rendered *excel, superabound.*)

II Corinthians 9:12, "**For the administration** of this service not only supplieth the **want** of the saints, but is abundant also by many thanksgivings unto God." (In this passage, the Greek word for the phrase "for the administration" is *diakonia*, which is co-equally rendered *official service, office, relief.* The Greek word for "want" is *husterma*, which is co-equally rendered *specifically poverty, that which was lacking.*)

If we are lacking ANYTHING that pertains to this life or Godliness, we need to follow the steps of God's relief service, and it becomes a natural reality of a Godly truth. His truth is that He has already given us ALL things that pertain to life and Godliness!

II Corinthians 9:13, "By the experiment of this ministration they glorify God..."

The Christians of Corinth experimented with this administration (the instructions from God's Word for having their wants met) and they glorified God, because their *wants* were met.

GALATIANS

Galatians 2:16, "Knowing that a man is not **justified** (*dikaioo – innocent, holy*) by the works of the law, but by the **faith** of Jesus Christ..." (In this passage, the Greek word for "faith" is *pistis*, which is co-equally rendered *assurance, belief, evidence, authority, to rely by inward certainty: assure, believe, have confidence, be [wax] content, make friend, obey, persuade, trust, yield.*)

So, we are innocent, holy and justified, because we have belief, confidence and trust in God's Word.

Galatians 3:5, "He therefore that ministereth to you the Spirit, and worketh miracles among you, doeth it by the works of the law, or **by the hearing** of **faith** (*pistis*)?" (In this passage, the Greek word for the phrase "by the hearing" is *akoē*, which is co-equally rendered as *audience*.)

Today, we minister and work miracles in the Spirit because of trust, confidence and belief in God's Word. We have all of God's miracle-working power, because God has already given it to us, and we are simply using what He has given.

We receive faith by hearing or giving audience to God's Word. The best way to give audience to God's Word is to read It.

In Jeremiah 33:3 God's Word says, "**Call** unto Me, and I will answer thee, and shew thee great and **mighty** things, which thou knowest not." (In this passage, the Hebrew word for "call" is *qârâ'*, which is co-equally rendered *encounter*. The Hebrew word for "mighty" is *bâtsar,* which is co-equally rendered *inaccessible things*.)

If we will read God's Word and have an encounter with God, based upon His Word (coming to Him with our whole heart, Jeremiah 29:13), He will answer us and show us things that are inaccessible by any other way. We will experience the secret and mighty things of God! If you want to see great and mighty things beyond anything that you've ever imagined, **read until** God answers or speaks to you! **I am not using legalism to say "read to earn", instead I am saying "read to**

learn"! Reading God's Word is using God's power! If you only want a little of God's power, then just read a little.

Galatians 3:8, "...that God would justify the heathen through faith."

God has justified the entire human race. They simply need to receive it.

EPHESIANS

Ephesians 1:8, "Wherein He hath abounded toward us in all wisdom and **prudence**." (In this passage, the Greek word for "prudence" is *phronesis*, which is co-equally rendered *intellectual or moral insight.*)

Ephesians 1:9, "Having made known unto us mystery of His will."

We do not have to beg for God's will to be revealed. All we need to do is read His Word. I understand that God will sometimes lead us to do something that may not be plainly spelled out in His Word; however, He will never lead us to do something that would be contrary to His Word.

Ephesians 1:18-19, "The eyes of your understanding being enlightened; that ye may know what is the hope of His calling, and what the riches of the glory of His inheritance in the saints, and what is the exceeding greatness of His **power** (*dunamis*)."

We must pray that the eyes of our understanding be enlightened, so that we can know that God has already given us His power (the Apostle Paul prayed this prayer for the people of Asia Minor).

Ephesians 1:17-19, "That the God of our Lord Jesus Christ, the Father of Glory, may give unto you the spirit of wisdom and revelation in the knowledge of Him: The eyes of your understanding being enlightened; that yet may know what is the hope of His calling, and what the riches of the glory of His inheritance in the saints, And what is the exceeding greatness of His power to usward who believe, according to the working of His mighty power."

Ephesians 3:14-21, "For this cause I bow my knees unto the Father of our Lord Jesus Christ, of Whom the whole family in Heaven and earth is named, that He would grant you, according to the riches of His glory, to be strengthened with might by His Spirit in the inner man; that Christ may dwell in your hearts by faith; that ye, being rooted and grounded in love, may be able to comprehend with all saints what is the breadth, and length, and depth, and height; and to know the love of Christ, which passeth knowledge, that ye might be filled with all the fullness of God. Now unto Him that is able to do exceeding abundantly above all that we ask or think, according to the power that worketh in us, unto Him be glory in the church by Christ Jesus throughout all ages, world without end. Amen."

In 1977, I heard Brother Kenneth Hagin tell the story of how after pastoring for twelve or so years, the Lord showed him the Ephesians' prayer (Ephesians 1:17-19 and 3:14-21). He began to pray it at least once, daily. After about six months, it began to change his life and ministry, so much so that he looked back in amazement that he had not been fired from his position as pastor during the previous twelve years!

Since the first day I heard Brother Hagin tell this story, I began to pray this Ephesians' prayer, and in the years that followed, the Lord has taught me many things. Better than any human, the Holy Spirit can teach us His Word, show us that the Word of God is alive, give us understanding on verses having multiple meanings, all the while, maintaining accuracy of true Godly doctrine.

Ephesians 1:22-23, "And hath put all things under His feet, and gave him to be the head over all things to the church, which is His body, the fullness of Him that filleth all in all."

If the mind (the power) of God is going to be fulfilled in this world, the church is going to have to do it.

Ephesians 2:1, "And you hath He quickened who were dead in trespasses and sins..."

Ephesians 2:22, "In Whom ye also are builded together for a **habitation** of God through the Spirit." (In this passage, the Greek word for "habitation" is *ktoikētērion*, which is co-equally rendered *dwelling place, house permanently, to occupy a house*.)

We are ordained of God to live with this type of lifestyle (see Ephesians 2:10). God lives in us when Jesus Christ is the Lord of our lives and we are filled with the Holy Spirit with the evidence of speaking in tongues!

Ephesians 3:4, "Whereby, when ye read, ye may understand my knowledge in the **mystery** of Christ." (In this passage, the Greek word for "mystery" is *musterion*, which is co-equally rendered *secret*.)

When we read God's Word, we begin to understand the very secrets of God that has ALREADY BEEN GIVEN TO US!

Ephesians 3:19-20 is a powerful secret that belongs to us, "And to know the love of Christ, which passeth knowledge, that ye might be filled with all the fullness of God. Now unto Him that is able to do exceeding abundantly above all that we ask or think, according to the power that worketh in us" (see my book entitled, Unimaginable Love).

How powerful it is to be filled with all of the fullness of God. If we fully understand this verse, it opens the door for this truth to become a reality in our lives (I Thessalonians 2:13, "...it is the Word of God, which effectually worketh in us that believe.")

Ephesians 4:11-13, "And He gave some, apostles; and some, prophets; and some, evangelists; and some, pastors and teachers; For the perfecting of the saints, for the work of the ministry, for the edifying of the body of Christ: Till we all come into the unity of the faith, and of the knowledge of the Son of God, unto a perfect man, unto the measure of the stature of the fullness of Christ."

God gave ministries to perfect us until we are completely perfect as was Christ.

Ephesians 4:24, "And that ye put on the new man, which after God is created in righteousness and true holiness."

God gave us this position; *however, we must put it on.*

Ephesians 4:29, "Let no corrupt communication proceed out of your mouth, but that which is good to the use of edifying, that it may minister **grace**." (In this passage, the Greek word for "grace" is *charis*, which is co-equally rendered *especially the divine influence upon the heart and its reflection in the life, joy, pleasure, God speed, joy.*)

We can *choose* to be the actual mouthpiece of God, by speaking words that give divine influence into people's eternal spirits; words that give people divine life, divine blessings and divine joy. We have the honored position to be the mouthpiece of God!

Ephesians 5:17, "Wherefore, be ye not unwise, but understanding what the will of the Lord is."

God has given us the privilege and the commandment to understand God's will.

Ephesians 5:18, "...be filled with the Spirit."

In verse 19, God gives us the instruction of how to do this, "Speaking to yourselves in psalms and hymns and **spiritual** songs, singing and making melody in your heart to the Lord." (In this passage, the Greek word for "spiritual" is *pneumatikos*, which is co-equally rendered *[divinely] supernatural.*)

An illustration of being filled with the Holy Spirit with the evidence of speaking in tongues is like owning a huge generator. You can use it whenever you want to. All **you have to** do is turn it on (see Acts 2:4).

Ephesians 6:10, "Be strong in the Lord and in the power of His might."

If we make the decision, we can have God's power.

Ephesians 6:11, "Put on the whole armour of God!"

Ephesians 6:13, "Wherefore, take unto you the whole armour of God..."

Ephesians 6:16, "Above all, taking the shield of faith, wherewith ye shall be able to quench all the fiery darts of the wicked."

God has given us the ability to stop all of satan's attacks!

PHILIPPIANS

Philippians 1:10, "That ye may approve things that are excellent; that ye may be **sincere** and without **offense** till the day of Christ." (In this passage, the Greek word for "sincere" is *eilikrines,* which is co-equally rendered *pure.* The Greek word for "offense" in this passage is *aproskopos,* which is co-equally rendered *faultless.*)

We are pure and faultless!

Philippians 2:5-6, "Let this mind be in you, which was also in Christ Jesus: Who, being in the form of God, thought it not robbery to be equal with God."

Philippians 2:9-10, "...and given Him (*Jesus*) a name which is above every name: That at the name of Jesus every knee should bow, of things in Heaven, and things in earth, and things under the earth."

God gave us Jesus' name, which is above every name, more authority and power than any other name in existence. Every name that is contrary to God's goodness must bow and give reverence to the name of Jesus. God has given us the privilege to use the name of Jesus (see Ephesians 1:19-23).

Philippians 2:13, "For it is God which worketh in you!"

God is working in us; therefore, we have all of the power in existence working in us!

Philippians 2:15, "That ye may be blameless..."

We are blameless.

COLOSSIANS

In Colossians 1:9, Paul prayed the perfect will of God for the Colossian people, "For this cause, since the day we heard it, do not cease to pray for you, and to desire that ye might be filled with knowledge of His will in all wisdom and spiritual understanding."

God is no respecter of persons (see Acts 10:34). What He has done for one, He will do for all, as He is the same yesterday, today and forever (see Hebrews 13:8).

Colossians 1:10, "...increasing with the knowledge of God."

Colossians 1:11, "Strengthened with all might, according to His glorious **power** (*dunamis*)!

Colossians 1:26, "...the mystery now made manifest in saints."

Colossians 3:10, "...put on the new man after the image of God!"

Colossians 3:15, "And let the peace of God rule in your hearts."

The same peace that God has is ours. We do not have to work for it. All we have to do is LET it rule in our hearts and lives.

I THESSALONIANS

I Thessalonians 4:11-12, "...study that you would lack nothing."

I Thessalonians 5:5, "...we are children of **light** (*phos*)!"

We have the power from God streaming from us, because we are children of the light, children of God!

I Thessalonians 5:23, "...we are blameless!"

I TIMOTHY

I Timothy 4:15, "Meditate upon these things; give thyself wholly to them; that thy profiting may appear to all."

Meditation causes us to hear God's voice more clearly in order to receive instructions. Jesus paid the price for us to profit in every area of thinking (see John 14:26).

I Timothy 5:7, "And these things give in charge, that they may be blameless" (Notice in verse 5, God was giving instruction for verse 7 – to become blameless).

If God tells us that we can receive a blameless lifestyle, then we can.

I Timothy 6:11, "...**follow** after righteousness, Godliness..." (In this passage, the Greek word for "follow" is *diōkō*, which is co-equally rendered *pursue, press toward.*)

If God is telling us to pursue and press toward being righteous and God-like, then we can!

II TIMOTHY

II Timothy 1:6, "...**that thou stir** up the **gift** that is in thee." (In this passage, the Greek word for the phrase "that thou stir" is *anazōpureō*, which is co-equally rendered *to re-enkindle*. The Greek word for "gift" is *charisma*, which is co-equally rendered *divine passion; specifically a spiritual endowment, miraculous faculty*.)

Clearly, God has already given us His divine passion of spiritual endowment, His miraculous faculty. We simply MUST initiate this blessing for it to be in operation and manifested in this natural world.

II Timothy 1:7, "For God hath not given us the spirit of fear; but of **power** (*dunamis*), and of love, and of a sound mind."

II Timothy 2:21, "If a man therefore purge himself from these, he shall be a vessel unto honor, sanctified, and meet for the Master's use, and prepared unto every good work."

By simply reading the many passages of Scripture in this book, you can see the undeniable validation that God has already given us everything we could possibly need or desire in our natural and spiritual lives.

However, sin blinds the eyes of a person, and will keep them from receiving, because they cannot see or understand what God has given them.

As you study the whole chapter of II Timothy 2, you will see sin that we MUST purge from our lives, in order to see and understand the greatness of what God has given us.

TITUS

Titus 2:12, "Teaching us that, denying ungodliness and worldly lusts, we should live soberly, righteously, and Godly, in this present world."

If God's Word tells us we should live like Him, then we can!

Titus 2:11-12, "For the grace of God that bringeth salvation hath appeared to all men, teaching us that, denying ungodliness and worldly lusts, we should live soberly, righteously, and godly, in this present world."

Clearly righteousness and Godliness have been given to ALL humanity by God's grace, but we must deny ungodliness and worldly lusts in order for these things to be a reality in our natural lives. Sin allows satan to blind our eyes, keeping us from seeing or using what God has given us.

HEBREWS

Hebrews 3:6, "But Christ as a Son over his own house; whose house are we, if we hold fast the confidence and the rejoicing of the hope firm unto the end."

We are the house of God. He lives in us.

Hebrews 4:1, "Let us therefore **fear,** lest, a promise being left us of entering into His **rest**, any of you should seem to come short of it." (In this passage, the Greek word for "fear" is *phobeo,* which is co-equally rendered *exceedingly, reverence.* The Greek word for "rest" is *katapausis,* which is co-equally rendered *the Heavenly blessedness in which God dwells; which He has promised to believers in Christ.*)

Wow! According to God's Word, we can have a lifestyle of dwelling in the Heavenly blessedness in which God, Himself, dwells!

Hebrews 4:3, "For we which have believed do enter into rest..."

All we have to do is believe, act accordingly, and trust, in order to live in this rest!

Hebrews 4:9, "There remaineth therefore a rest to the people of God. "

Hebrews 4:11, "Let us **labor** therefore to enter into that rest..." (In this passage, the Greek word for "labor" is *spoudazo*, which is co-equally rendered *earnest, diligent study*.)

Hebrews 4:12, "For the Word of God is quick and powerful..."

We have been given God's powerful Word!

Hebrews 4:16, "Let us therefore come boldly to the throne of grace..."

God has already given us the privilege to be able to come to the throne of God any time we desire!

Hebrews 5:12, "We can teach the oracles of God!

In Hebrews 6:5, we learn that we can taste of the **powers** (*dunamis*) of the world to come!

Hebrews 6:12, "That ye not be slothful, but follower of them who through faith and patience inherit the promises."

Hebrews 8:6, "But now hath He obtained a more excellent ministry, by how much also He is the mediator of a better covenant, which was established upon better promises."

Anything God did for people in the Old Testament will be done for us, and more!

Hebrews 10:35-36, "Cast not away therefore your confidence, which hath great recompense of reward. For ye have need of patience, that, after ye have done the will of God, ye might receive **the promise**." (In this passage, the Greek word for the phrase "the promise" is *epaggelia*, which is co-equally rendered *especially a divine assurance of good: message, promise.*)

Today, when we receive, it is not because God initiates anything for us; it is because WE initiate our faith and patience.

JAMES

James 1:12, "Blessed is the man that endureth temptations: for when he is tried, he shall receive the crown of life, which the Lord hath promised to them that love Him."

We must initiate endurance to receive what the Lord has already given us.

James 1:18, "Of His own will begat He us with the word of truth, that we should be a kind of first-fruits of His creatures."

James 1:25, "But whoso looketh into the perfect law of liberty, and continueth therein, he being not a forgetful hearer, but a doer of the work, this man shall be blessed (*fortunate, happy*) in his deed."

James 2:9 says that if anyone (*this includes God, proving He doesn't pick favorites*) chooses one over another, they are in sin. We do not receive blessings because God has reached down and chosen someone to be blessed over another. Rather, because we "initiate looking into the perfect law of liberty, and continue therein."

James 2:24, "Ye see then how that by **works** a man is **justified** (*dikaioo*) and not by faith only." (In this passage, the Greek word for "works" is *ergon*, which is co-equally rendered *actions.*)

The person that initiates corresponding actions to God's Word becomes justified, innocent and holy.

I PETER

I Peter 2:9, "But ye are a chosen generation, a **royal** priesthood, a holy nation, a peculiar people; that ye should show forth the praises of Him Who hath called you out of darkness into His marvelous **light** (*phos*)." (In this passage, the Greek word for "royal" is *basilios*, whose root meaning is *a foundation of power.*)

We have already been chosen and called by God to do this ministry, now it is up to us to do it (see my book entitled, Releasing God's Anointing)!

I Peter 2:24, "...by His stripes, we **WERE healed**." (In this passage, the Greek word for the phrase "were healed" is *iaomai,* which is co-equally rendered *cure, make whole.*)

In the mind of God, when Jesus died on the cross, He paid for healing and wholeness in our bodies, minds and spirits. It is up to us to accept this, as we must initiate this healing that has been given to us (see Romans 8:32).

I Peter 3:10, "For he that will love life, and see good days, let him refrain his tongue from evil, and his lips that they speak no guile."

If we want to love life and see good days, we must make this decision to initiate the action of choosing to refrain our tongues from speaking evil and deceit. Great people are not born, they are made!

I Peter 4:1, "Forasmuch then as Christ hath **suffered** for us in the flesh, arm yourselves likewise with the same mind: for he that hath **suffered** in the flesh hath ceased from sin." (In this passage, the Greek word for "suffered" is *pascho,* which is co-equally rendered *to experience a sensation or impression [usually painful].*)

Sin is when our flesh wants to do something that is contrary to God's Word. There is pleasure in all sin, but the wages are a 99% detriment to us (see Romans

6:23). However, there is a sensation of pain when we MAKE our flesh obey the Word of God. An example of this would be the strong sensations and longings for tobacco that a person experiences, when they try to quit after years of smoking tobacco.

The more we introduce our bodies to sin, the more our bodies suffer when we withdraw from that sin. We must remember the flesh has NO sense; it must be trained. The flesh is neither spirit nor intellect. If we allow our flesh to control us, we will be sinful people and will reap horrible wages. When we sin, it gives satan rights to give us his wages. Satan is not fair, so he will always give us the wages that we do not deserve – death.

The divine side of this passage is that when Christ defeated sin, He paid the price for us to share this same victory; however, we must initiate this action. The people of the Old Testament did not have this privilege, as they could not control their flesh or cease from sinning. They had no resisting power, and you can read of the many sinful acts of numerous good people in the Old Testament.

I Peter 4:11, "If any man speak, let him speak as the oracles of God, if any man minister, let him do it as of the ability which God giveth: that God in all things may be glorified through Jesus Christ, to Whom be praise and dominion forever and ever. Amen."

We must initiate *speaking the very oracles of God.* Simply put, when we choose to speak only things that are in agreement with God's Word, we are speaking oracles of God (see Ephesians 4:29).

I Peter 5:6, "Humble yourselves therefore under the mighty hand of God, that He may exalt **you in due** time." (In this passage, the Greek word for the phrase "you in due" is *idios*, which is co-equally rendered *proper.*)

So, WE MUST initiate humility, as this activates God's exaltation for us. God will not make us humble, we must make this choice.

I Peter 5:7, "Casting all your care upon Him: for He careth for you."

We must cast our cares on the Lord. He is not going to take them from us.

I Peter 5:8-9, "BE sober, BE vigilant; because your adversary the devil, as a roaring lion, walketh about, seeking whom he may devour: Whom resist steadfast in the faith..."

If we want victory over the devil, WE MUST CHOOSE to be sober, vigilant and steadfast in the faith. God is not going to do anything about the devil bothering us. He has already given us everything we need to be victorious over the devil. God will speak to us, guide us and bring His Word to our remembrance, but we must activate God's power that He has given us.

II PETER

II Peter 1:4, "Whereby are given unto us exceeding great and precious promises: that by these ye might be partakers of the divine nature, having escaped the corruption that is in the world through lust."

Notice II Peter 1:5-7 tells us that by our diligence, we are to add to our faith, knowledge, temperance, patience, Godliness, brotherly kindness and charity. We should never ask God to give us these things, because He has already done so.

We must search the Scriptures to find ways of conducting ourselves with these qualities. We have to train our flesh to act according to God's Word.

The devil has used the following deceptive, demonic doctrine for thousands of years, "Ask God to do it for you, and if you do not get it, it is not God's will for you to have it." Along with the spirit of deception comes a lazy, demonic spirit that says, "If I can put all of the responsibility on God, then I can just set back and do nothing. I am just waiting on God." When in fact, God is waiting on us to take and accept what He has given.

II Peter 3:18, "But GROW in grace and in the knowledge of our Lord and Savior Jesus Christ..."

You are the understood subject of this verse. *You* grow in grace and knowledge. We can pray for more grace, but God will not give us any, because He has already given us more grace than we could ever possibly use. With purpose, we must accept grace and walk in His grace. We must read His Word to grow in knowledge. **God is our helper, not our worker!**

I JOHN

I John 1:7, "But if **we walk** in the **light** (*phos*) as He is in the **light** (*phos*), we have fellowship one with another and the blood of Jesus Christ His Son cleanseth us from all sin." (In this passage, the Greek word for the phrase "we walk" is *peripateo*, which is co-equally rendered *deport oneself.*)

We must choose to put spiritual, mental and physical actions towards walking in God's light. We have the awesome privilege to walk and live in the same kind of miracle light as God, Himself, walks and lives.

I John 2:5, "But whoso keepeth His word, in Him verily is the love of God perfected: hereby know we that we are in Him."

When WE CHOOSE to keep God's Word in use, His love is automatically perfected in us.

II Peter 2:9, "The Lord knoweth how to deliver the Godly out of temptations."

We are "the Godly".

I John 2:10, "He that loveth his brother (countryman) abideth in the **light** (*phos*), and there is none occasion of stumbling in him."

If you do not want to make any mistakes, deliberately begin to love everyone.

I John 2:17, "...he that doeth the will of God abideth for ever."

The person that purposely does the will of God will live forever!

I John 2:27, "But the anointing which ye have received of Him abideth in you."

God has already given us His anointing. Take it!

I John 2:29, "...every one that DOETH righteousness is born of Him."

I John 3:1, "Behold, what manner of love the Father hath bestowed upon us, that we should be called the sons of God."

Even though we are all God's children, many do not know this and therefore will not believe it, thus missing eternity in Heaven.

I John 3:2, "Beloved, now we are the sons of God."

I John 3:3, "And every man that hath this hope in Him purifieth himself, even as He is pure."

If we want to be as pure as the Lord, Himself, all we have to do is have hope that God is telling us the truth. Once we have hope, we then read the Word of God. Then, we do not need hope any longer, as we mature to faith (a knowing).

I John 3:6, "Whosoever abideth in Him sinneth not."

If we want to be in a place of life where we do not sin anymore, we must learn to purposely abide in God and His Word, which are the same.

I John 3:9, "Whosoever is born of God doth not commit sin; for his seed remaineth in Him: and he cannot sin, because he is born of God."

Keep in mind that the sin mentioned in this verse is talking about the sin of rejecting Jesus as Lord. As long as Jesus is your Lord, you are not committing this sin.

As you study the Scriptures, you will find that there are three categories of sin:

- The first category is rejecting Jesus Christ as your Lord and Savoir (You can be forgiven of this sin, if you accept Jesus as your Lord).
- The second is blasphemy of the Holy Spirit (No one can be forgiven of saying, "There is no God," after they have already been filled with the Holy Spirit, with the evidence of speaking in tongues and operated with all of the Gifts of the Holy Spirit, Hebrews 6:4-6.)
- The last category of sin is everything else, from speaking idle words to murder. (A person can be forgiven of all of these sins, if they repent.) This last category of sin causes some people to think that because they have not *rejected* Jesus as their Lord, they can live with sin in their lives and still go to Heaven. However, all sin grows up to the point of rejecting Jesus as Lord. James 1:15 says that when sin is finished, it brings death. When we continue to allow sin to be a part of our lives without trying to remove it, we are actually rejecting Jesus as Lord. Rejecting the Word of God, concerning what sin is and how to be free from it, is in fact, rejecting Jesus, because the Word of God is Jesus (see John 6:63).

I John 4:4, "...greater is He that is in you than he that is in the world."

I John 4:7, "...everyone that loveth is born of God, and knoweth God."

When we make the step of allowing God's unconditional love to rule in our lives, we know we are born to God (a child of God with eternal divine life, now being the major part of us), and we get the awesome privilege of getting to know God.

I John 4:12, "...If we love one another, God dwelleth in us, and His love is perfected in us."

When we allow God's unconditional love to rule in our lives, God lives inside of our spirits, and His love (all of His miracle power) is perfected in us.

I John 4:15, "Whosoever shall **confess** that Jesus is the Son of God, God dwelleth in him, and he in God." (In this passage, the Greek word for "confess" is *homologeo,* which is co-equally rendered *covenant, promise.*)

When a person takes the initiative to confess that Jesus is the Son of God, God lives in them.

I John 4:16, "...God is love; and he that dwelleth in love, dwelleth in God, and God in him."

The decision is ours. If we choose to let unconditional love live in us, we will actually have God in all of His fullness living inside of us!

I John 4:17, "...because as He is, so are we in this world."

The person that initiates and allows love to rule in their life is likened unto God.

I John 4:18, "There is no fear in love."

The person that allows God's unconditional love to rule in them will never fear ANYTHING.

I John 5:1, "Whosoever **believeth** that Jesus is the Christ is born of God." (In this passage, the Greek word for "believeth" is *pisteuo*, which is co-equally rendered *commit, trust, have faith.*)

When a person believes in Christ, they are born of God. This "believing" is something a person must initiate.

I John 5:4, "...this is the victory that over-cometh the world, even our **faith**." (In this passage, the Greek word for "faith" is *pistis*, which is co-equally rendered *assurance, belief.*)

If we have real Bible faith, we will initiate some spiritual, mental and physical actions (see James 2:20).

I John 5:14-15, "And this is the confidence that we have in Him, that if we ask anything according to His will, He heareth us. And if we know that He hears us, whatsoever we ask, we know that we have the petitions that we desired of Him..."

When we pray to the Lord in agreement with His Word, He hears us, and verse 15 says that **God hearing us is equivalent to us receiving our petitions!**

III JOHN

III John 1:2, "Beloved, I wish above all things that thou mayest prosper and be in health, even as thy **soul** prospereth." (In this passage, the Greek word for "soul" is *psoo-khay*, which is co-equally rendered *from mind.*)

III John 1:4, "I have no greater joy than to hear that my children **walk** in truth. (In this passage, the Greek word for "walk" is *peripateo*, which is co-equally rendered *to tread all around, to live, deport oneself, be occupied with, tread under foot.*)

The word "walk" in this passage clearly gives spiritual, physical and mental actions to God's Word. Keep in mind, God's Word is the highest order of truth (see John 17:17).

The summation of verses 2 and 4 is that **God's truth (His Word) says that He has no greater joy, knowing**

that we (His children) experience personal and financial prosperity and health.

JUDE

Jude 1:20, "But ye, beloved, building up yourselves on your most holy faith, praying in the Holy Ghost."

If we want to build up ourselves, we MUST take the initiative to pray in the Holy Ghost.

REVELATION

Revelation 1:3, "Blessed is he that readeth."

God has already given His Word. Receiving God's Word is reading it.

Revelation 1:5-6, "...Unto Him that loved us, and washed us from our sins in His own blood and hath made us kings and priests unto God."

Revelation 3:11, "...hold that fast which thou hast that no man take thy **crown**." (In this passage, the Greek word for "crown" is *stephanos*, which is co-equally rendered *a crown of royalty and honor*.)

God has given us crowns of life, indicating that we can reign as kings in this life (see Romans 5:17). When someone has been crowned with royalty and honor, they are entitled the best of that kingdom. We've been crowned to be kings and queens of the Kingdom of Heaven. So, by God's command, we are entitled to the best that God's Kingdom (Heaven) has. It has been given to us; however, *we must* hold fast! God is not going to do this for us; it is up to us.

Revelation 5:10, "And hast made us unto our God kings and priests: and we shall **reign** on the earth." (In this passage, the Greek word for "reign" is *basileuō*, which is co-equally rendered *to rule as a king, with a foundation of power.*)

This verse is reflecting back on the redeemed work of Christ; the work that Christ did to make us kings and priests to reign on this earth.

Revelation 12:11, "And they overcame him by the blood of the Lamb, and by the word of their testimony; and they loved not their lives unto the death."

This prophetic passage is telling us that there will be Christians who will overcome satan and his kingdom by their initiated efforts of trusting the promises that have been paid for by Jesus' death and by speaking (and standing on) God's Word. This is the people born-again from the resurrection of Jesus until the rapture of the church.

Revelation 17:14, "...the Lamb shall overcome them: for He is Lord of lords, and King of kings."

We are the "kings" of whom Jesus is the "King of" (see Romans 5:17)!

Revelation 21:7, "He that overcometh shall inherit all things; and I will be his God, and he shall be My son."

IF WE CHOOSE to take God's Word and overcome evil with the power of His goodness, then we shall inherit all things. Again, God will help us, but we must do the action.

Revelation 22:7, "...blessed is he that keepeth the sayings of the prophecy of this book."

The blessings have been given, but we must choose to keep them.

CHAPTER 10

TAKING WHAT BELONGS TO YOU

We must know and receive God's truth, before the blessings (that God has already given us) can be a reality in our natural and spiritual lives.

With a very relaxed state of mind and body, a person who takes what belongs to them knows what God's Word says and accepts it as truth. Only after they have relaxed (yielded, accepted the truth), would they apply audible and physical actions (acting like the Word of God is truth). Then the spiritual, mental and natural manifestations of God's Word would become a reality that can be seen with the eyes or touched with the hands.

KNOWING THE TRUTH

What does it truly mean to know God's Word?

In Hosea 4:6, God tells us that His people are destroyed for a lack of knowledge. If we do not **know** the truth of what God has for us, we cannot enjoy those truths.

In John 8:32, Jesus said, "And ye shall **know** the **truth**, and the **truth** shall make you free." (In this passage, the Greek word for "know" is *ginōskō*, which is co-equally rendered *allow, be aware (of), feel, (have) known (-ledge), perceive, can speak, be sure, understand*. The Greek word for "truth" is *aletheia,* referenced throughout the Scriptures to *God's Word.*) (see John 14:6, 17; 15:26; 17:17; Romans 1:18, 25; II Corinthians 6:7; Galatians 2:5, 14; Ephesians 1:13; I Timothy 2:4 and II Timothy 2:15)

To know the truth in the way that Jesus meant, we would need to *allow* God's Word (truth) to be in our lives, allow ourselves to *feel* God's Word, *speak* God's Word and spend time *meditating* and *studying* God's Word, until we *understand* what It is saying.

To *know* God's Word, we must first read or hear It, and then apply the full meaning of the Word "know" into our lives.

UNDERSTANDING THE NAME OF JESUS

John 1:1, "In the beginning was the Word, and the Word was with God, and the Word was God."

John 1:14, "And the Word was made flesh, and dwelt among us, (and we beheld His glory, the glory as of the only begotten of the Father) full of grace and truth."

Revelation 19:13, "And He was clothed with a vesture dipped in blood: and His name is called The Word of God."

I John 5:7, "...for there are three that bear record in Heaven, the Father, the Word, and the Holy Ghost: and these three are One."

The Bible teaches us that Jesus' name is above all names (see Philippians 2:9; Ephesians 1:20-23).

YIELD, THEN ACT

Receiving God's Word (after you have a mental knowledge of what it says) takes **two steps**:

- Surrender/yield to God's Word
- Display natural actions of accepting God's Word

BE STILL

Surrendering and yielding to God's Word is literally relaxing in one's mind and body. The Greek word for "yield" is *paristēmi*, which is co-equally rendered *present, lay, horizontal posture, properly reflexive and utterly prostrate, conceive*.

In Romans 6:19, God's Word teaches us, "for as ye have yielded your members (limb/part of the body) to uncleanness and to iniquity unto iniquity; even so now yield your members servants to **righteousness** unto **holiness**." (In this passage, the Greek word for "righteousness" is *dikaiosunē*, which is co-equally rendered *innocent, absolutely*. The Greek word for "holiness" is *hagiasmos*, which is co-equally rendered *purification, physically pure, morally blameless.*)

Through His Word, God is telling us that just as easily as we have yielded/surrendered our bodily parts to sin, it is just as easy to yield to God's righteousness and His holiness.

In order for a person to yield, they would need to relax that part of their body (or that part of their life) to receive God's Word (power) (see Romans 1:16).

I Thessalonians 4:11-12, "**And that ye study** and to do your own business, and to work with your own hands, as we commanded you; That ye may walk honestly toward them that are without, and that ye may have lack of nothing." (In this passage, the Greek word for the phrase "and that ye study" is *philotimeomai*, which is co-equally rendered *eagerly and earnestly study; to be quiet [rest, refrain from labor; conceive].*)

If we will eagerly and earnestly study God's Word to find out what belongs to us, conceive the Word into our minds and spirits (by resting, refraining from any kind of labor, relaxing), we will be in a position where we lack nothing. This is the first step of receiving God's Word.

Psalm 46:10, "**Be still**, and know that I am God: I will be exalted among the heathen, I will be exalted in the earth." (In this passage, the Hebrew word for the phrase "be still" is *râphâh*, which is co-equally rendered *cease, faint, be feeble, idle, be weak; to cure, cause to heal, physician, repair, make whole.*)

If we will learn to cease our physical and mental strain, we can experience God's healing, wholeness and physical repair in our bodies (and God will be exalted in all of the earth).

Just the other day, I stopped to ask a man for directions. The man was holding his back and had a look of pain on his face. When I asked what was wrong, he filled his sentences with curses and explained his need for a doctor due to his back pain. When I told him that God loved him and that I could pray for him to receive healing, he gave me a strange look as if to say, “You’ve got to be kidding!” I told him that I was only going to lay my hand on his back and pray. He replied, "Well, I guess it can’t hurt anything."

I laid my hand on his back, and told the pain and the ill will to leave in Jesus’ name. Then, I commanded that area of his back to *relax* and receive God's relief. I then asked him to twist his back from side to side. He grinned and said, "Where did you learn to do that?" He then looked at my hands, as if I had something in them (only the same things as all other Christians, the sunlight splendor of God’s miracle-working power, see Mark 16:18).

I have witnessed greater miracles, such as blinded eyes opening, deaf ears opening, recreated deformities and the dead rising to life again, etc. And it is all done in the same simple way that I prayed for this man’s back. As we learn to relax, surrender and yield to God's power, the world will exalt God.

Exodus 14:13, “And Moses said unto the people, Fear **ye not, stand** still, and see **the salvation** of the Lord, which He show to you today.” (In this passage, the Hebrew word for the phrase "ye not stand" is *yâtsab,* which is co-equally rendered *reflexively, act in an uncontrolled manner.* The Hebrew word for the phrase "the salvation" is *yshu ah,* which is rendered *deliverance, victory, prosperity, health.)*

Moses, along with the people of God, witnessed the supernatural salvation of God (one of the greatest miracles in the Bible), because they surrendered, yielded to an uncontrolled manner; they relaxed.

NOW, ACT!

If there are no actions, our faith, our belief is dead. We must have *energetic forceful actions*, which is seen in Matthew 11:12, "And from the days of John the Baptist until now the kingdom of heaven **suffereth violence, and the violent** take it by force." (In this passage, the Greek word for the phrase "suffereth violence" is *biazō*, which is co-equally rendered *to force, press, vital activity, violence.* The Greek word for the phrase "and the violent" is *biastēs*, which is co-equally rendered *energetic force, violence, vital activity.*)

In Matthew 16:19, Jesus said that the keys of the kingdom of heaven are given to us, and in Matthew 3:2, that the kingdom of heaven is at hand. If you have keys to something, you can enter in a locked domain. And if something is at hand, it is close enough for you to take.

If we want these blessings, we must spiritually, mentally, physically, energetically and forcefully take what God has already given. You *mentally* read the Scriptures, then *spiritually* accept them into your spirit (the foundation of your person), and then *physically* take it with your whole heart.

James 2:19 teaches us that the devils in hell believe in God, which is why in the very next verse God's Word tells us that we must have **works** (*ergon*) with our **faith** (*pistis*). If we do not, our faith is dead. If we say that we believe God and His Word, but have no corresponding actions, then our faith, our belief in God and His Word is as that of the devils, because even the devils of hell believe in God and His Word, but they will not act in love, forgiveness, kindness, etc. In other words, the devils of hell do not have corresponding actions of their belief in God or His Word.

ACTIONS PRODUCE MANIFESTATIONS

Luke 16:16, "...since that time the Kingdom of God is preached, and every **man presseth** into it." (In this passage, the Greek word for the phrase "man presseth" is *biaziō*, which is the same Greek word for "violence" in Matthew 11:12, and is co-equally rendered *to force, suffer violence, through the idea of vital activity*.)

Since the time of the Old Testament, **EVERYONE** that has entered the blessings of the Kingdom of God on this earth has done so because they have pressed into it!

If we are not energetically and vitally having actions to God's promises, then we are not going to have them.

THE WOMAN WITH THE ISSUE OF BLOOD

In Matthew 9 and Luke 8, we find the story of the lady who had a blood disease for twelve years, and after spending all of her money on doctors, only grew worse. The woman said within herself, "If I may but touch His garment, I shall be whole." This insinuates that she was crawling, as the hem nearly touched the ground.

When I was 27 years old, I contracted an incurable blood disease. Only the Word of God and my application of the truths that I've included in this book made me totally whole in less than 2 weeks. I shared this with you to let you know that I am familiar with the type of symptoms this lady was fighting. She must have said, "Today is going to be a new day for me. I am taking my healing."

You will notice in this passage that Jesus never prayed for her, touched her or even preached to her. She energetically and forcefully took her healing. She took what belonged to her.

In Luke 8:45, Jesus said, "Who touched me?" Peter answered, "Master, the multitude throng thee and press thee, and sayest thou, Who touched me?"

Jesus replied, "**Virtue** (*dunamis*) is gone out of me."

This lady initiated this miracle. She took what belonged to her. Actions activated God's greatest miracle-working power!

PETER WALKS ON WATER

In Matthew 14, you will find the story of Jesus walking on the water out to the midst of the sea towards His disciples.

"When the disciples saw Jesus, they were troubled, saying, It is a spirit: and they cried out for fear. Jesus said, Be of good cheer; it is I; be not afraid. Peter answered Him and said, Lord, if it be Thou, bid me come unto Thee on the water."

Jesus did not pray for, lay hands on or preach Peter a message on how to walk on water. He spoke only one word, "Come."

Peter responded by getting out of the boat and walking on the water. He initiated this miracle by getting out of his comfort zone. He had to get out of his boat and ignore great men of God that were in the boat (notice: all the disciples were given the instruction, yet only one acted on it, thus receiving the miracle).

THE MAN WITH THE WITHERED HAND

In Mark 3:1-5, you will find another story of a man that initiated God's power by his actions, "And He entered again into the synagogue; and there was a man there which had a **withered** hand." (The Greek word for "withered" is *ērainō*, which co-equally rendered *dried up, shrunken.*)

In verse 5, we see that Jesus did not touch or pray for him, "...He saith unto the man, Stretch forth thine hand. **And he stretched** it out: and his hand was restored whole as the other." (The Greek word for "and he stretched" is *ekteinō*, which is co-equally rendered *actions, exceedingly, heartly.*)

BLIND BARTIMAEUS

In Mark 10:46-52, Bartimaeus heard that Jesus was walking by, and he "sat by the highway side begging. And when he heard that it was Jesus of Nazareth, he began **to cry** out, and say, Jesus thou Son of David, have mercy on me. And many charged him that he should hold his peace: but he cried the more a great deal, Thou Son of David, have mercy on me. And Jesus stood still, and commanded him to be called. And they call the blind man, saying unto him, Be of good comfort, rise; He calleth thee. **And he, casting** away his garment, rose, and came to Jesus." (In this passage, the Greek word for the phrase "to cry" is *krazō*, which is co-equally rendered *to scream, shriek, exclaim, to call aloud*. The Greek word for the phrase "and he casting" is *apoballō*, whose foundational words are *violent or intense casting down.*)

Bartimaeus heard about this miracle-worker (Jesus), and regardless of the opposition against him, he shrieked and screamed until he got Jesus' attention. When Jesus told him to come to Him, Bartimaeus forcefully threw away his garment (which was his security blanket, as in those days a cloak was issued by the government to the blind as a license to beg for a means of living), and he came to Jesus.

Bartimaeus was taking his new beginning. He had extreme, determined actions that screamed, "Today, is a new day for me!" He was saying, "I am tired of being blind, and today, I will see!"

Continuing on from verse 51, "And Jesus answered and said unto him, What wilt thou that I should do unto thee? The blind man said unto Him, Lord, that I might receive my sight. And Jesus said unto him, Go thy way; thy faith hath made thee whole. And immediately he received his sight, and followed Jesus in the way."

Bartimaeus' miracle did not come when he first yielded, surrendered, and relaxed to God's words. His miracle did not come when he had just actions. His miracle took place **after** he yielded and acted.

MODERN DAY EXAMPLES

Philippians 4:13, "**I can do** all things through Christ which **strengtheneth** me." (In this passage, the Greek word for the phrase, "I can do" is *ischuō*, which is co-equally rendered *to exercise force, be much work*. The Greek word for "strengtheneth" is *endunamoō*, which is co-equally rendered *empower*, with the root word *dunamis*.)

As we do everything we can possibly do, spiritually, mentally and physically, the activating, miracle-working power of God comes into manifestation and a miracle in the natural realm is known!

I was 18 years old and in the Army, when I bought my first car that was worth anything. I was so proud and took such good care of that 2 year-old 6-cylinder Mustang. Late one evening in a rough area of town near the base at Fort Riley, Kansas, I found a rack to drive the car up on, in order to change the oil. As I was pulling my car up onto the rack, my left front tire went off, causing it to hang in mid-air. I climbed out of the car broken-hearted, as this car meant so much to me. It was the only earthly possession that I owned, and I knew it would be vandalized if I had to leave it overnight. Philippians 4:13 came to mind, as I climbed underneath the car. I simply believed every word. I believed that the same God Who worked with Samson, would not only work with and through me spiritually, but also physically. So, I found an old board on the ground and placed it across the bottom of the car. I pushed with everything I had, but it felt like I was trying to lift up a mountain. Then a supernatural strength came alive inside of me. The weight of the car almost felt like nothing, and I put the car back upon the rack.

Many years later in 1991, I went to one of the poorest parts of Monterrey, Mexico, to hold a miracle crusade for the people who lived there. When I called for people with deformities to come up on the platform, a lady in her early thirties responded. She had a large hump on her back that physically bent her over about 30 degrees. I asked her to sit on a chair on the platform, and saw that her legs were uneven by about 6 inches, as well. I released God's power into her spirit, mind and body. **She began to force her leg to grow out, to force her body straight** with all of her ability. Within seconds, her leg grew out completely, and her body straightened out. She jumped up and began to praise the Lord.

A few evenings later, a man was brought into the meeting that had been recently ran over by a vehicle. Someone had previously attempted to help him by pushing his protruding thighbone back in place through an open wound. The lacerations were still bare and bleeding as they carried this man, moaning loudly with pain, to the meeting on a stretcher. I prayed for him in the same way that I had prayed for the lady who was deformed. After I finished praying for him, I told him to do something that he could not do before. He stopped moaning, got off of the stretcher, and free from pain, walked out of sight, totally normal without even the slightest limp.

Many miracles took place in that crusade, which caused an atmosphere for many to accept Jesus Christ as their Lord and Savior.

Jeremiah 1:12, "Then said the LORD unto me, Thou hast well seen: for I will **hasten my Word** to perform it." (In this passage, the Hebrew word for "hasten" is *shaqad,* which is co-equally rendered *watch, sleepless.* The Hebrew word for the phrase "my word" is *dabar,* which is co-equally rendered *as spoken of, act, task, thing done, work.*)

God sleeplessly watches over His Word! He is not watching over the letter, the Word that is only sitting on a table or in someone's mind who refuses to act like It is true. The letter kills, but the Spirit gives life (see I Corinthians 3:6). When a person gives life to God's Word, God gives Spirit to It!

People miss the awesomeness of God by crying and pleading for God to do something. But God has already given them ALL THINGS THAT PERTAIN TO THIS LIFE AND GODLINESS (II Peter 1:3-4)!

We know the truth of what God's Word says, so, we can command the evil situation to leave in the name of Jesus. We learn to relax/yield/surrender spiritually, mentally and physically (instructing the person who we are ministering to, to do the same), then, instruct them to have energetic, forceful actions spiritually, mentally and physically.

CHAPTER 11

(If God has already given everything that pertains to life and Godliness, then...)

WHY SHOULD WE PRAY?

Many people have confused prayer with begging or petitioning for something from God. The major foundation and purpose of prayer is to communicate with our loving Heavenly Father. Prayer is primarily for fellowship.

When we are in a time of need, as we fellowship with the Lord, He will bring to our remembrance what He has already given us, along with Scripture to use for that which we are believing (John 14:26).

Our time of prayer and fellowship with God is when He may inform us of spiritual warfare, remind us of a Scripture (to activate our finances, show us actions we should take in agreement with His Word concerning an area of concern in our lives, remind us to be consistent in speaking in agreement with His Word, or show us where we need to forgive) in order to allow His power to work for us (Mark 11:25).

While we are fellowshipping with Him (praying), He gives us instructions of things that we may need to do in order to have a natural manifestation of a spiritual blessing that He has already given to us. The richest miracle is to know the Lord!

The Apostle Paul had the wonderful privilege of knowing the Lord. He realized that the more you know Him, the more there is to know about Him. After the Apostle Paul had seen blinded eyes opened, deaf ears to hear, the crippled to walk, the incurable cured, the dead to rise to life again, etc., he experienced seeing Jesus in visions and was translated to Heaven. And after all of that, he made the statement, "That I may know Him" (Philippians 3:10).

We can only experience this supernatural lifestyle when we pray (fellowship) to our Heavenly Father. This is a contentment and fulfillment that the world knows nothing about. This relationship with the Lord (that you only get through prayer) is so rich that everything can be going wrong (in the natural), yet you still have a smile on your face, because of the contentment and tranquil peace (that passes all knowledge) in your heart.

John 14:27, "Peace I leave with you, My peace I give unto you: not as the world giveth, give I unto you."

CLOSING

The purpose of this book is to give confidence and boldness to the believer, as they learn how to take action for the things that rightfully belong to them because of the price Jesus paid on the cross.

Deuteronomy 29:29, "The secret things belong unto the Lord our God: BUT those things which are **revealed** BELONG UNTO US AND TO OUR CHILDREN FOR EVER, THAT WE MANY DO ALL THE WORDS OF THIS LAW!" (In this passage, the Hebrew word for "revealed" is *galah,* which is co-equally rendered *plainly published.*)

Resources by Mel Bond

The Nine Gifts Of The Holy Spirit Belong To You!

God's Last Days' People

Neglecting Signs & Wonders Is Neglecting The Rapture

Why Jesus Appears To People Today

Understanding Your Worst Enemy

Heaven Declares Christians' Greatest Problem

If It's Not Good, It's Not God

Releasing God's Anointing

Unimaginable Love

How To See In The Spirit World

Come Up Higher (Donna's cd)